ECHOES OF AN ANCIENT FOREST

By WILLIAM CROSSING

(With an Introduction by Brian Le Messurier)

FOREST PUBLISHING

First published in 1994 by FOREST PUBLISHING, Woodstock, Liverton, Newton Abbot, Devon TQ12 6JJ

British Library Cataloguing in Publication Data

A catalogue record for this book is available from the British Library.

ISBN 0–9515274–4–4

Forest Publishing

Editorial, design and layout, and colour photography by:
Mike Lang

Typeset by:
Carnaby Typesetting, Torquay, Devon TQ1 1EG

Printed and bound in Great Britain by:
The Latimer Trend Group, Plymouth, Devon PL6 7PL

Cover photographs:

Front – Wistman's Wood, in the valley of the West Dart

Back – The interior of Wistman's Wood

CONTENTS

ACKNOWLEDGEMENTS

The Publishers wish to sincerely thank all of those people who have provided assistance during the compilation of this book.

Particular thanks are due to Mr. Colin Davison, Editor of *The Western Morning News*; to Mr. Brian Le Messurier for writing the Introduction; to Lady Sylvia Sayer for allowing us to reproduce her drawing of the twelve knights and their retainers at Nun's (Siward's) Cross during the Perambulation of 1240; to Miss Elisabeth Stanbrook for kindly providing most of the photographs which add so much to this book.

LIST OF ILLUSTRATIONS

INTRODUCTION

The series of articles now published in book form for the first time was written when William Crossing was earning his living from the pen. From being the manager of the family canvas mill, his circumstances changed so that he was forced to be a full-time scribe, turning his Dartmoor knowledge and experience into an income of sorts, but he was always short of money. Who was he, and what were the events which led to him writing 'Echoes of an Ancient forest'?

William Crossing was born in Plymouth on 14 November 1847 and spent much of his boyhood in that city. As a child he was encouraged by his mother to interest himself in the antiquities and traditions of the countryside, and since the family spent holidays in a cottage on Roborough Down he was introduced to Dartmoor at an early age.

When he left school he was apprenticed to a sail-cloth manufacturer, but, disliking the trade, ran away to sea and sailed to Canada. By the time he was twenty he had returned to Plymouth and was working for his father. In his spare time he wrote poetry and plays, and also took every opportunity to visit the moor which remained his chief interest.

Mr Crossing senior, no doubt feeling that a position of responsibility would benefit his son, sent William to supervise the family mill at South Brent. But away from parental control William indulged in his twin delights of drama and Dartmoor more freely than ever; he ran a local theatre, which after an initial success failed financially, and the moor was at his doorstep.

Theatricals continued to attract, and so William formed his own professional drama group with which he went on tour. When this venture failed, too, he returned to the South Brent mill, which his long-suffering father had kept going, and resumed his Dartmoor explorations. Perhaps because of his lack of interest it was not long before the canvas mill closed down, and he was left struggling for his livelihood. It is worth remembering, however, that with the development of steam propulsion at sea the need for ships' sails would have diminished.

He had married in 1872 and shortly afterwards began to keep careful records of his Dartmoor excursions and studies. With no desire to return to business he determined to earn his daily bread by writing, but he and his wife, Emma, stayed on at South Brent until the 1890s, when they moved to Brent Tor, and then to Mary Tavy. Until the end of the century, when his health began to deteriorate, Crossing constantly walked or rode the moor, never shirking a soaking in his tweed clothes and leather gaiters. Wherever he went he made friends with the moormen, and he was a popular figure in the group round the peat fire in the evenings, when he would play tunes on his tin whistle, or recite an improvised rhyme describing his wanderings of the day.

Crossing had joined the Dartmoor Preservation Association soon after it was formed in 1883, and was a member of the Devonshire Association from 1881 to 1891, although he never contributed to the *Transactions* of that body. From being a person of some substance – he writes in *Amid Devonia's Alps* of having 'a man' called George in 1872 – he became so impoverished that he had to resign from both Associations.

He now wrote an extended article for *Doidge's Western Counties Illustrated Annual* for 1892 called 'The Land of Steam and Tor'. This almanac-type publication came out each year about Christmas time, so he would have written it in 1891. One feels it was prepared with a view to separate and simultaneous publication as a small book about Dartmoor, for it appeared under its own covers as *The Land of Steam and Tor* by William Crossing with the following words on the title page:

Re-printed (by permission) from

Doidge's Western Counties Illustrated Annual for 1892

For Private Circulation Only

1891

This book is also issued concurrently by Forest Publishing for the first time in 102 years.

By 1893 one senses he was finding it difficult to make ends meet. From now until the end of the century he found such literary employment as he could, but this was a relatively barren period of his life. His health had deteriorated, and he was compelled to remain at home for long spells. He became editor of *The Westcountry Annual*, brought out a small book called *Cricket Averages* and other unexpected titles like *Mount Edgecumbe Souvenir*, *The Book of Fair Devon* and *The Marine and River Guide to the South Coast of Devon and Cornwall.*

With the end of the nineteenth century he saw his opportunity to write a series of articles telling the story of the hundred years just past in so far as they affected Dartmoor. Thus 'A Hundred Years on Dartmoor' began its seventeen-week run in *The Western Morning News* in June 1900. These articles were published a year later in book form with the addition of photographs and several appendices. (It is a matter of interest that the book carried the words *One Hundred Years ...* on the cover, but *A Hundred Years ...* on the title page). The book was highly successful and went into five editions.

Thus it was on the success of *A Hundred Years ...* that Crossing was engaged to write 'Echoes of an Ancient Forest'. On the 29 October 1901 *The Western Morning News* printed the following paragraphs:

William Crossing as he was in about 1895. The drawing is a copy of a photograph in *West-Country Poets*, 1896, and first appeared in *The Western Morning News* in 1904.

Echoes of an Ancient Forest

We have pleasure in announcing that we shall in a few days begin the publication of a further series of articles, under the above title, by Mr William Crossing, whose *One Hundred Years on Dartmoor* has proved so popular both in serial and in book form.

The series about to begin will trace the various waymarks in Dartmoor history from the time of King John down to the close of the eighteenth century, at which point the volume now in its third edition takes up the story.

This was followed on the 1 November 1901 by the first weekly article which was introduced as follows:

We publish today the first of a series of special articles entitled 'Echoes of an Ancient Forest' by Mr William Crossing, author of *One Hundred Years on Dartmoor*.

Reading between the lines, one suspects that 'Echoes...' was commissioned by *The Western Morning News* with a view to later publication as a book, like *One Hundred Years* ..., but this never happened. Certainly 'Echoes ...' is not a typical William Crossing piece. It gives the initial impression of being more a history of Dartmoor, and indeed it is a major contribution to that end. But it is far more than that as his essays on the Perambulation, the Lands of Isabella de Fortibus, the Reeves and the Foresters, and so on are all written from the point of view of one who knows the places he is discussing. He brings history and topography together in the style of the true all-rounder. He certainly had mud on his boots, but he burnt the midnight oil as well.

It is worth quoting an exchange of letters which occurred during the publication of the series. Under the heading 'Echoes of an Ancient Forest' the following letter was published on 25 January 1902:

> Sir, I notice in the Dartmoor article of today's *Western Morning News* Mr Crossing mentions that 'the cross at Buckland Ford has disappeared'. If I can throw any light on this matter I shall be only too pleased. Between 40 and 50 years ago Lady Littler (who was then residing at Bigadon, the former seat of the late Richard John King) placed an old Dartmoor cross in Buckfastleigh churchyard to the memory of one of her family. Whether or no this cross is the missing Buckland Ford cross I am not in a position to say, but as a boy I remember it was said that Lady Littler had no right to use the cross, as it was purchased by the late Richard King from some moormen, and that he intended to erect it in its proper position. Probably the reason why this was not done was that Mr King had to give up the Bigadon property, and the cross was left behind. The cross that I allude to is, I consider, at present in Buckfastleigh churchyard.
>
> Observans

A reply was sent by Crossing to the newspaper on the same day which reads:

> Sir, I have read with very much interest the account which 'Observans' gives of the old cross in Buckfastleigh churchyard. While its connection with the one said to have been erected at Buckland Ford in 1557 is not actually apparent there is nothing improbable in the supposition that it is the same. My belief is that the cross mentioned by the jury of survey as marking at the ford the boundary which they claimed was not one then made for that purpose, but was probably taken from some place in the vicinity, where it had served to point out the direction of the Abbots' Way. We can hardly suppose that its original site on the monks' path was at Buckland Ford, for that spot is so near Huntingdon Cross that it would scarcely have been needed. It is more likely that it stood originally on the ridge to the westward, midway between Petre's Cross and Red Lake Mire.
>
> My searches for the cross commenced some time in the 1870s, and I made many enquiries then of those who had known the locality for a number of years – two of them had worked at the peat beds nearby before 1850 – but I could never glean any tidings of it. The information furnished by 'Observans' I am glad to receive, as it opens up new ground which I shall not fail to explore.

I may mention that in the account of the inquisition on the Brent Moor boundary in Dr Oliver's *Monasticon Diocesis Exoniensis* it is stated that each of the crosses bore the words 'Bunda de Brentmore'. No such inscription is, however, to be found on the three that remain on the moor.
William Crossing
West Black Down, Dartmoor
25 January

It is likely that some of Crossing's statements have been overtaken by subsequent scholarship; a detailed critique has not been undertaken. The articles are printed here as written by Crossing. His spelling of place-names is retained, but certain details are amended for the sake of consistency and present-day typographic correctness.

Numerous other articles by Crossing followed, and a glance at his list of writings in *The Dartmoor Bibliography* (compiled by Peter Hamilton-Leggett, Devon Books, 1992) shows his incredible output at this time.

In 1906 he became tutor to the three sons of Mr W. P. Collins, and teaching was carried on alongside work on his magnum opus, the *Guide to Dartmoor*. This went into three editions, and has been reprinted in recent years.

Crossing's last years are touched with sadness. Mr Collins arranged a public subscription for him on his 70th birthday, but shortly afterwards the old couple had to move to Ivybridge, where relations lived, for Mrs Crossing was ailing. When constant nursing became necessary she was admitted to Tavistock Institution (the workhouse in common parlance), and she died there on 6 June 1921.

Mr Collins found accommodation for his old friend at Mary Tavy, and Crossing lived there for a while. In 1924, while he was away from home, the woman who looked after his rooms found a mass of papers and, because mice had damaged them, burnt the lot. Since Crossing had been preparing a history of Dartmoor, and the notes represented a lifetime's work, the loss was irreplaceable. For twelve weeks from 9 July 1925 he was a patient at Tavistock Institution, but in October he was taken to Cross Park Nursing Home, in Plymouth, where he spent his last three years. During this time Mr Collins paid the bills, which amounted to several hundred pounds. While at Cross Park he published his last book, a volume of poems called *Cranmere*, after the principal work it contained. His first book, *Leaves from Sherwood* (1868) was also poetry.

William Crossing died on 3 September 1928, and is buried with his wife in Mary Tavy churchyard. The grave is north-east of the church, and standing by it one can see the western slopes of Dartmoor swelling up less than a mile away.

Our debt to Crossing is enormous. He was the pioneer of a rational study of Dartmoor. He discovered stone crosses whose whereabouts had long been forgotten, and recorded their position in his books on the subject. He was the accurate chronicler of customs now gone from the country calendar, and his collection of folklore tales was made before the memory of them was lost forever. He gained the confidence and respect of Dartmoor people and from them learned the obscure place-names, and as the result of frequent forays across the whole of the moor acquired a minute knowledge of every hill and valley, and many of the antiquities which had been the subject of unproven theorising. He can be relied upon to present the true Dartmoor, unadorned by flights of fancy. It is good that a wider public can read his words once more, for although written so long ago, they have stood the test of time.

Brian Le Messurier
August 1994

✻✻✻✻✻

I

HOW THE MEN OF DEVON FREED THEIR COUNTY FROM THE FOREST LAWS

While Dartmoor possesses much to interest the archaeologist, it is certainly not deficient in that which will engage the attention of the student of local history.

Though long regarded as barren, not only in respect of its soil, but as being incapable of yielding a reward to those who might seek to unlock its story, it will be found upon investigation to be by no means so. Its annals reveal it as the field of the operations of the medieval tinner, as the country of the old-time franklin, and as the region where long lingered many of the usages of the ancient Forest, and these having no existence in Devonshire outside the confines of the moor give to it a history of its own.

Although we do not hear of Dartmoor by name until the beginning of the 13th century, when it was reserved as a Forest, or hunting-ground, by King John, there is evidence tending to shew that not only was it an appanage of the Crown a hundred years before that time, but that it also formed part of the possessions of the Norman Conqueror. Indeed it is probable that the moor was even earlier Royal demesne, and was devoted to the purposes of the chase by the Saxon Kings, for the Forests of England had their origin at a very remote period. Manwood, who, in the reign of Elizabeth, wrote a treatise on the Laws of the Forest, says 'it doth not appear, either by histories or records,' when they were first formed; and also tells us that they were 'oulie for kings, princes, and great, worthie parsonages; and not for meane men of mean calling or condition.'

The record to which we usually turn for information concerning the early state of a place does not help us when we seek to know something of Dartmoor, for in the Domesday Survey it is not even mentioned. But Lydford, with which the great waste has always been connected, is named therein, and as we learn from it that the borough, as it then was, was held by the King, there is no reason to doubt that he possessed the moor also. That such is not stated is no proof to the contrary, for Dartmoor would not be likely to be enumerated among the lands entered in Domesday. It has been pointed out that only such as were productive and capable of bearing a tax were noticed in that survey, and consequently uncultivated tracts of land do not find a place there.

William, when apportioning the spoils of his victory, retained for himself all those lands which had been the property of Harold, and those which had belonged to the Crown. Dartmoor, there is little doubt, became his as having formed part of the possessions of the latter.

If the laws of the chase had been harsh in the time of the Saxon Kings, they were incomparably more so under Norman rule. They are set forth, or otherwise noticed, in the work by Manwood, already referred to; in the *Familiar Letters* by Howell; in Coke's *Institutes*; as well as in the writings of Maine, Lindwode, Ockam, and others.

From these we learn some of the penalties for 'Forest breach'. If it could be proved against any man that he had disabled a wild animal, his goods were confiscated, and he was imprisoned. His eyes were put out if the animal chanced to be a stag, buck, or boar, and if a stag was killed the slayer was to suffer death. Even free-men who possessed land of their own were not permitted to hunt on it unless they first obtained the King's permission. No man was allowed into a forest at night, and such persons as were expected to keep the paths in repair were subject to penalties if they neglected their duties, as by so doing they might cause wayfarers to turn aside from them, and so disturb the game. Heavy punishment was meted out to those who destroyed cover, and even on their own land no-one might cut wood, except in the presence of a forester. There was nothing that bore so heavily upon the people as these oppressive laws, and it is little to be wondered at that when they grew in strength they should seek to be freed from them.

During all the stormy years that followed the appearance of the Norman on the shores of England, these cruel laws were in operation. The whole county of Devon was under them, and her children knew no rest. In Henry II's reign the penalties for offences against them were not quite so severe as formerly, the prison was substituted for the gallows, but otherwise there was little amendment. Throughout the country complaints arose. Large tracts of land had been turned into Royal Forests, for the King had power to erect any portion of his waste lands into such, and over the counties in which these were situated the Forest Laws operated. The murmurings of the people were for long unheeded, but at length there were indications in the Westcountry that their voice had been heard.

The spirit which animated the Western men in England's golden age was born at a period long anterior to that stirring time, for it was manifested in the days of Norman tyranny. They stood foremost among those who were determined to throw off the yoke imposed upon them. In 1217 the Charter of Forests was granted (though but little effect was given to it), by which all lands throughout England, except Royal Demesne, were disafforested, and were thus no longer to be subject to the obnoxious laws. But 13 years before that time the men of Devon had demanded to be freed from their operation. In 1204 they forced a charter from the King, which disafforested the whole of their county with the exception of the waste of Dartmoor. The Charter of Forests was obtained from King John by the might of the people of England; that of 1204 was wrung from the same monarch by the Devonshire men alone.

Before the close of the 12th century John had by charter confirmed to the earls, barons, knights, and to all free tenants, clergy, and laity in Devon their liberties of the Forest, which they had in the time of Henry I, and which permitted them to carry bows and arrows, and to kill deer and other wild animals specified, on their own lands *outside* the bounds of the Forest. This seems to show that complaints from Devon had reached the ears of John, and that he deemed it expedient to endeavour to pacify the free tenants in the county, though in reality he merely confirmed rights to which they had long been entitled, and did nothing to remove that from which they actually suffered. The charter, which is in the possession of the Dean and Chapter of Exeter, was granted before John ascended the Throne, in 1199, for in it he is styled the Earl of Mortaigne, and not King of England. It is probable that he was then holding the Forest under grant from the Crown.

Although Dartmoor is not mentioned by name in this charter, it certainly is by implication, for the Forest referred to can be none other than that. This is, indeed, clearly shown in the charter of 1204.

John also granted in 1201, in the second year of his reign, a charter to the tinners, who possessed rights on Dartmoor, it being one of their privileges to 'dig tin and turf for smelting tin everywhere in the lands, the moors, and the wastes,' whether belonging to the King or to other persons. That John endeavoured to conciliate the men of the West there is certainly room for supposing.

But the relief afforded by these concessions, if such they may be called, was very slight. Although the Forest Laws may not have been so severe as in the early Norman times, they were yet very harsh, and such as could not be borne by men who were beginning to learn what freedom was. The men of Devon banded together, bent upon redress, and brought their grievances before the King. It is probable that John, convinced of their determination to be rid of the yoke which pressed so heavily upon them, deemed it wise to yield with a good grace to their demands. But he was not disposed to accede to them without a quid pro quo; it was not his way to be a party to a bargain where the benefit would be all on one side, unless that side happened to be his. He would consent to disafforest the county, reserving only his own demesne, on condition that the people paid a fine of 5,000 marks.

Doubtless the men of Devon thought this would be money well spent. To free their province from the hated laws, quietly and effectually, was a most desirable object, and worth the sum demanded. The terms were agreed to.

On the 18th day of May, 1204, the charter for disafforesting the county of Devon was signed at Winchester, the witnesses being the Lord Herbert, Bishop of Salisbury; Geoffrey FitzPeter, Earl of Essex; Baldwin, Earl of Albermarle; William, Earl Ferrars; Henry, Earl of Hereford; William de Braosa; Hugo de Nevill; William Briwere; and Simon de Tateshull. In the charter John declares that he has 'disafforested all Devon of all things appertaining to the Forest and

Foresters, unto the bounds of the ancient regards of Dertmore and Exemore, which regards were in the time of King Henry the First.'

The charter provides that the men of Devon and their heirs for ever should retain their rights in the two moors named, which rights were undoubtedly those of pasturage and turbary. These are spoken of as having been enjoyed by the men of the county so far back as the time of Henry I, and in return for them they were to continue to render certain services, as had been the custom then. It was to be lawful for anyone to clear away cover, to make parks, to have bows and arrows and all other kinds of arms, to keep dogs, and to engage in the chase, outside the bounds of Dartmoor and Exmoor. Within those bounds none of this was to be permitted; those moors were to remain the special hunting grounds of the King.

There are other provisions in the charter relative to the time at which the Sheriff of Devon was to hold his inquiries in the county concerning pleas of the Crown, and other things which belonged to the Crown, and also on the matter of bailing prisoners.

These clauses make it only too clear that the people of Devon had suffered serious abuses at the hands of those who, placed in authority over them, found in the harsh laws of the time a means by which they were able to gratify a spirit of revenge or to extort money.

There are some important points regarding Dartmoor in this charter. In the first place, we learn that the bounds of the Forest in 1204 were the same as those recognised a century earlier, and, in the second, that the men of Devon possessed rights of common upon the moor which were in existence in the time of Henry I. Further, we find that not only did the people of the county seek to be freed from the operation of the Forest Laws, and to obtain redress in other directions, but that they were at the same time regardful of their common rights on the moor.

With respect to Exmoor being mentioned in the charter, it may be well to explain that although that part of it which, until comparatively recent times, formed the ancient Forest of that name, lies wholly within the county of Somerset, some portion of its purlieus, or surrounding commons, are in Devonshire. At the date of the charter it is certain that these common lands extended far into the latter county, cultivation having greatly curtailed their area.

It is not improbable that in John's reign the regards of Exmoor Forest either ran into Devon or were for a short distance conterminous with the boundary of that county. The rights of the men of Devon over Exmoor named in the charter, it is likely, were exercised on its western purlieus only.

With the charter of 1204 the history of Dartmoor begins, though we learn little of it during the remaining years of John. The charter, itself, was kept in Tavistock Abbey, together with a confirmation of it by Henry III, and was afterwards copied into the register of Walter Stapeldon, Bishop of Exeter.

No sooner had John granted the charter than he set about collecting the fine which the men of Devon had agreed to pay. Persons were appointed for this duty, and, as we learn from the Close Rolls, were enjoined to use all diligence in their work. The charter was signed on the 18th May, and on the 4th July, just over 6 weeks later, Rogo Fitzsimon and Philip de Lega paid 300 marks of silver (£200) on account of the fine at Dorchester. By the end of the third year after the grant the 5,000 marks were paid.

But though the men of Devon fulfilled their part of the bargain, it certainly does not appear that the King carried out his. He exhibited far greater alacrity in collecting his money than in keeping his promise. It is more than doubtful whether the provision of his charter ever took effect. There is no record of the Forest bounds having been viewed at the time it was granted, and by the Forest Laws it was necessary that these should be perambulated before disafforestation could take place.

It is true that in a writ of the fourth of Henry III, commanding the Sheriff of Devon to permit Roger de Toeny to hold his land in Dartmoor in peace, there is mention of a perambulation having been made in the time of John. But it is uncertain whether such was not named merely on the authority of De Toeny, who says that he (or his father may perhaps be meant) had seizen of his land by that perambulation; or it is possible that the so-called 'perambulation' was simply a viewing of the bounds of De Toeny's holding.

But however this may be, and while it appears that the men of Devon failed to obtain by the charter of John that for which they had striven, it is quite certain that the rights, both of the commoners and the tinners, continued to be recognised. We find from the Close Rolls that a little later there were disputes between the Forest officers and certain landholders as to the rights of the latter in the Forest, but the Sheriff of Devon is commanded by writ to see that they were permitted to hold their land in peace.

That King John neglected to put the provisions of his charter into force was no doubt a great disappointment to those who had done so much to obtain it, and he who once advised that no trust should be placed in princes probably rose in their estimation as a man of experience. But their labour was not altogether in vain. The first steps had been taken, and though not leading them to freedom, had brought them some way towards it. They had shewn an example to the country, and probably caused men to think, and to look about them for some means of escape from tyranny. Others may earlier have sought to disafforest tracts of land – indeed, the charter seems to shew that such was the case – but here a whole county, and that the third in England in size, had by the exertions of its inhabitants been rendered exempt from the Forest Laws, the reward only being lost to those who had struggled for their freedom through a Monarch failing to keep his promise.

In the Charter of Forests which John was compelled to grant in 1217, soon after he had signed the Great Charter, the language of one clause, it has been observed, is so like that employed in the Devon charter of 1204 as to lead to the supposition that one was based upon the other. The charter to the men of

Devon did not free their county as they had hoped, but had it never been forced from the King the ultimate victory over oppression might have come even later than it did.

The associations of the old, wild Forest of Dartmoor with the efforts for freedom made by those who were reared in the smiling land around it are not among the least to be treasured. When Devon's sons bestirred themselves in the cause of liberty the light began to penetrate the darkness that had too long rested on the land. The sun of hope was about to rise, and to cheer a nation by its rays. The husbandman and the peasant were no longer to be reckoned as being of less account than the beasts of the Forest. The toiler on the land was to have his rights recognised, not those alone pertaining to the hunting ground of Monarchs, but his rights as a man.

II

THE PERAMBULATION OF 1240

It is the month of July, and the old moor wears its summer garb. As yet the heather has not purpled the hills, only tinged them with a dull red, but the furze has long since burst into bloom, and more than one border height rises, as it were, from a sea of gold. The tiny leaves of the whortleberry are fresh and green, and where the plants are thickest half shroud the masses of weather-stained granite that lie in confused heaps upon the slopes. Cattle and ragged-looking ponies graze upon the short, sweet grass, growing in patches amid the heather on which the dewdrops yet hang, for it is early morn. A silence rests upon the moor, broken only by the rustling of the tall bracken in the hollows, as the gentle breeze sweeps over it, or by the sound of waters in their never-ceasing flow.

On the high enclosed Taw plain, and near the river's brink, are heaps of stones and debris, showing where the tinners delved for the coveted ore. But the hour at which his daily labour should commence goes by, and he is not seen; the sun mounts higher in the heavens, but there is no sign of his coming. By and bye the priour, in whose charge are the flocks and herds in this part of the Forest, rides hastily up the valley. Usually he spends much time in examining the beasts, but this morning he has evidently none to spare, for after a few minutes' observation he appears to be satisfied that all is well, and turns his pony's head towards the in-ground. It is clear that today there is something afoot, which is drawing men from the scene of their daily avocations. Let us follow the herdsman down the valley, and learn what it is.

As he approaches the lower, or northern, end of Taw Plain, a herd of ponies is seen galloping over the heath as though disturbed by something unusual, and the cattle feeding on the higher ground raise their heads and look steadily towards that part of the valley above which rise the rugged Belstone tors. Then they, too, seem to take the alarm, and turning hastily seek the further end of the secluded level through which the Taw lazily rolls. A short distance further, and the priour comes in sight of the narrow entrance to the Belstone Cleave, and in another minute is aware that before him is a great concourse of men. Some are fording the river, while many have already passed over, and are streaming up the shoulder of Cosdon. It is the day appointed by the Sheriff of Devon for perambulating the bounds of the Forest of Dartmoor according to the command of

King Henry III and the knights chosen to view the bounds are about to set out.

Dartmoor remained a Royal Forest for only 35 years after we first hear of it by name. In 1239 Henry III, by charter, dated 10th October, bestowed upon his brother Richard, Earl of Cornwall, the Manor and Castle of Lydford, together with the Forest of Dartmoor, the earl to pay £10 yearly for the same. There being no special grant conveying to him the power to hold Forest Courts, without which warrant a subject cannot do so, Dartmoor ceased to be a Forest, and became in law a chase. Its disafforestation took place, therefore, by the operation of the grant of it to a subject. It is important to note that this change did not in any way affect the rights of the commoners, or of the tinners, on the moor.

But though the constitution of the courts held in connection with Dartmoor underwent a change on its becoming parcel of the earldom of Cornwall, they continued for a long period to bear among other titles that of the 'Court of the Forest.' We also find that the moor is sometimes referred to as a Forest, and at others as a chase, and we can understand why this is so. When there was no heir-apparent to the lordship of Dartmoor the Crown became its custodian, and received its revenues until the lordship was revived in the person of an Earl, or later, a Duke of Cornwall. The moor does not recover its original status and again become a Forest on reverting to the King, but through this occasional attachment to the Crown it has never lost that title.

As we have no very strong evidence of a perambulation of the moor being made in the time of John, either after his charter to the men of Devon, or following the later Charter of the Forest, it has been supposed that the first one directed by the King was made in 1224 under a statute passed in that year for perambulating, confirmatory of disafforestation, most of the Forests in England. Although there is no record of the fact, it is more than probable that the moor was perambulated at that time, as it would be necessary that such should be done in order to give effect to the provisions of the statute.

The first perambulation of Dartmoor of which we can speak with certainty, was made, not for the purpose of confirming disafforestation, but in order to determine the boundary between the Earl of Cornwall's new possession and those of the lords of the various manors surrounding it. This we learn from the writ of the King directing the perambulation to be made. It was witnessed at Westminster on 13th June 1240 and the perambulation took place in the following month.

The writ informed the Sheriff of Devon that 'our well-beloved brother, Richard, Earl of Poiteau and Cornwall,' had, with four knights who acted on behalf of the knights and free tenants holding lands adjoining the Forest of Dartmoor, submitted themselves to a perambulation of the boundaries of their possessions. The four knights thus representing the manorial lords were Henry de Merton, Hamel de Endon, Robert de Halyun and William le Pruz. The Sheriff was directed to choose twelve loyal knights of the county, and to go with them to the Forest, 'and by their oath cause the perambulation to be made between the aforesaid Forest and the aforesaid lands.'

The official return to this writ, by which the King was to be informed under the seals of the Sheriff and of four of the knights who had joined in the perambulation, by what metes and bounds it had been made, has not been discovered. There are, however, several copies of it in existence, and except for slight differences in the forms of some of the place-names, they may be said to agree. The returns state that the perambulation was made on the Eve of St. James the Apostle – the 24th July – in the 24th of Henry III. But it is not probable that the Forest boundary was viewed in one day; the distance to be traversed would be not far short of 50 miles, and this alone would need a longer time. There must also have been frequent stoppages in order to note the various bond-marks and settle any differences that might arise. The duties of the perambulators were not such as could be hurriedly discharged. It is therefore more than likely that the journey round the Forest extended over several days. Indeed, a tradition said to have formerly existed on the moor tends to confirm this view. A spot which we shall presently notice used to be pointed out as the resting-place of the perambulators during the first night of their journey. It seems not unreasonable to conclude that the date on the return to the writ was that on which the perambulation was completed.

The knights began their journey round the Forest at Cosdon, a hill in the north-east of the moor, but on what part of it the return to the writ does not inform us. At present the hill is regarded as being outside the Forest boundary line, and within the parish of South Tawton, but that it was wholly so in 1240 is not at all probable. The Sheriff and the knights say that they began their perambulation 'ad hogam de Cossdonne' – at the hill of Cosdon – and if they had commenced their bound-viewing on the line which is now considered to be the limit of South Tawton parish, and which has between it and Cosdon a stream known as Small Brook, and an eminence called White Hill, they would certainly not have mentioned Cosdon at all. It is reasonable to suppose that they would have stated that they began their perambulation on the Taw, at a point where a little stream falls into it. But they distinctly say that they began it at the hill of Cosdon, and it is therefore impossible to come to any other conclusion than that the bounds as then existing are not quite the same as those claimed by South Tawton today; that the parish has, in fact, thrust back the line marking the limits of the Forest. And this has been done by many parishes abutting on it.

But it is not intended here to discuss the question of the alterations in the Forest boundary line that may have taken place since the 13th century. We may, indeed, have to offer an occasional remark on the subject, but our chief purpose is to describe, in a circuit of the Forest, such of the bond-marks as can be readily identified with those named in the return made by the Sheriff of Devon, and the four knights, and to which they set their seals on the Eve of St. James the Apostle 1240.

There are few heights on Dartmoor commanding a wider and more varied view than Cosdon. From its lofty summit the eye wanders over the whole of the northern part of Devon, where the range of vision is bounded by the 'Severn Sea' off Barnstaple Bay, and the hills of Exmoor. Much of the eastern part of the county, and a considerable area of West Somerset is also seen, while southward a glimpse of the English Channel is visible, the view thus embracing the breadth of Devon from sea to sea. Woods and fields, farmsteads and villages and towns, are dotted over this vast extent of country, and though not a sound strikes upon the ear of the beholder, nor is a movement seen, the whole speaks of life. But when we turn and look down over Cosdon's slope, how is all changed. There we see nothing but desolation. The wild moor stretches far away, grim and silent, till its frowning hills soften against the distant sky.

On the very summit of the hill is a huge cairn, and other remains of a bygone age, grey and weather-beaten. In medieval times upon this point of vantage the signal fires were lit, and it is known as Cosdon Beacon to this day. Often the name is rendered Cawsand, and it is easy to see how this occurs. In the Devonshire vernaculary the 'd' would not be sounded. We have an instance of this in a document of the early part of the 17th century, in which the name is rendered Cosson.

The hill rises immediately above the village of Sticklepath, which offers itself as a convenient point from which to make the ascent of it. The village is situated on the road from Okehampton to Exeter, and is about 3½ miles distant from the former place.

There is a large concourse of people on the side of Cosdon on this July morning, of the year 1240. The twelve perambulators, and the four knights representing the manorial lords, and the Sheriff, have each their attendants, and there are clerks ready to note down the bond-marks as they shall be passed. Numbers of men have come from the borders, and many are yet seen flocking to the hill. The franklin from his homestead in the combe where the sycamores grow is there, and the villein who has cast aside the implements of husbandry, that he may betake him to the moor today to see those who shall view the bounds of the earl's land, which is to be no more Forest. There, too, are the foresters, in their doublets of green, who will henceforth take the place of the verderers, for these will be no longer known now that Dartmoor has become a chase. Priours are there, who have charge of the cattle agisted on the moor, and mounted on their native ponies, will be of much service as guides to the party throughout their journey of the ambit of the ancient Forest.

Many in that company are richly dressed, as befits their station, and others are clad in garb of a more sober sort, while the peasant wears his rough, untanned jerkin of sheepskin. And the habiliments of the men do not vary in their quality and style more than do the harness and the housings of the steeds, for well-groomed horses with ornamented saddles, and trappings of embossed leather, press the turf in company with unkempt ponies having nothing but a rude halter of cowhide. The scene is full of life as men throng towards the spot where stands the Sheriff in the midst of the knights, and for once the silence of the old moor is broken.

But they are already moving, and the foresters and the priours tell those around them, who have drawn back to allow the Sheriff and the perambulators to pass, that the Forest line runs from Cosdon to Hound Tor, a pile of rocks from which the ground on one side slopes down to a marsh out of which oozes a little feeder of the Teign. Slowly they pass onward, and the horsemen, and those on foot, follow them in one great throng until the tor is reached, and there they halt.

There is nothing particularly striking in Hound Tor itself, which is described in the return to the King's writ as 'parvam hogam' – a little hill – but it is remarkably well-placed on a ridge, and from it there is commanded an uninterrupted view of a large extent of moor. Here the parish of Throwleigh meets the Forest, the common lands belonging to which form, as it were, a long strip of ground, running out from the cultivated country between the commons of South Tawton and Gidleigh.

On the north-west side of the hill on which the tor stands is a rough track, used by the country-people for carting peat and rushes from the Forest. It runs from the enclosures above Prospect Place, near South Zeal, to the upper waters of the Steeperton Brook, a considerable tributary of the Taw. By means of this track the central parts of the Forest are easily reached.

It has been suggested that the tor to which the perambulators bent their steps from Cosdon was not that which we now call Hound Tor, but was another pile, two miles distant in a north-easterly direction. This is named Shilstone Tor, and stands on the verge of the common, in the parish of Throwleigh. There is no evidence that the perambulators ever went near it, but it was fixed as a possible bond-mark by those who have sought to shew that the Forest was once very much larger than it now is. To do this it became necessary to affix certain of the boundary names found in the Sheriff's return to the writ to objects that lie at some distance outside the recognised Forest line. But these objects bear names quite different to those mentioned in the return, and there is absolutely nothing to shew that they were ever called by any others. Until some evidence is forthcoming to prove that they were, and also that the objects regarded as bond-marks during several centuries did not bear their present names in 1240, there is no reason for supposing that the Forest boundary as now recognised differs very materially from that recorded by the perambulators in the reign of Henry III. At the same time nothing is more certain than that encroachments have been made upon the Forest by the parishes encircling it. But for the most part such are not extensive. When we come to notice the commons that form the purlieus of the Forest, we shall see that it is not probable that the latter has been greatly reduced in size.

The boundary named by the perambulators as the next in succession to Hound Tor is Thurlestone, and here again differences of opinion have arisen as to what object was intended by the name. But the identification of it with the northernmost pile of Watern Tor, the bond-mark recognised by the venville commoners, appears to us to present no difficulty whatever. To this rock-pile the name of Thurlestone now attaches, and were it not for a certain passage in the return made by a jury of survey who viewed the bounds of the Forest in 1609, its identification would probably never have been called in question. The jury trace the boundary line from Hound Tor to 'a place named in the said records (i.e., the older perambulations) Thurlestone, now, as they suppose, called Waterdontorr.' As they are only able to 'suppose' that Thurlestone was identical with Waterdon Tor, it would appear as though no part of the cluster of rocks was known by the former name at the period of their visit. But that Waterdon, or Watern Tor, as we now call it, was then regarded as a Forest bond-mark is certain, for we cannot suppose that the jury would return it as such without good and sufficient reason. They were making a survey of the moor, not to fix upon new boundaries, but to view existing ones, which it is only reasonable to suppose were known to the commoners living in their respective vicinities. Whether the rock-pile forming part of Watern Tor was at that time called Thurlestone or not is, therefore, not material. Nevertheless, that the jury were right in supposing the tor to be the same as that which was so called by the older perambulators, there can scarcely be a doubt. Evidence of this is afforded by the tor itself.

On the shore of Bigbury Bay is a remarkable rock, standing alone on the beach, and washed by the waves. It forms a natural arch, and is known as Thurlestone Rock, and gives name to the parish in which it is included. In the Devonshire vernacular 'drill' becomes 'dirl', thus a perforated stone or mass of rock becomes a 'dirlstone.' It is, therefore, easy to see the derivation of the name.

Thurlestone, Watern Tor

Now, viewed from certain points, Watern Tor presents a counterpart of the rock in Bigbury Bay. The northern pile rises from the turf at a distance of several feet from the central mass, but its overhanging summit approaches so closely to the latter that, except on a near view, the two have the appearance of a single rock pierced with an arch. The tor forms one of the curious features of the district, and it is told with truth upon the moor how a man may ride through the opening. That this rock should formerly be known as Thurlestone seems most fitting and we can scarcely come to any other conclusion than that we see in it the bond-mark named in the perambulation of 1240.

The commoners of Gidleigh, the parish which here abuts upon the Forest, consider that Thurlestone, or Watern Tor, which is the same thing, is the true bond-mark and it would probably surprise most of them to learn that a doubt had been cast upon the matter. Some in that neighbourhood may remember a dispute with the Duchy authorities respecting a part of the moor now within the enclosures of Teign Head Farm, but this related to ground southward of Watern Tor and did not affect that bound. But while Thurlestone has for centuries been regarded as being on the line marking the limits of the Forest, and the commoners of Gidleigh have always visited it when viewing their bounds, which they trace thither from a point known as Wild Tor Well, we have reason to believe that the Duchy authorities do not recognise Thurlestone as being a Forest bond-mark. Were access to the records in the Duchy office permitted, much light might be thrown on this and similar matters. But this is denied, and evidence has therefore to be obtained from other sources.

We do not think we are wrong in stating that the Duchy trace the line of the Forest from Hound Tor to Stone Tor Hill, a low eminence on Shovel Down, and to which is also given, according to documentary evidence which we possess, the name of Thurstone. The line is drawn straight between the points named, and runs through Battery Meres, otherwise Batworthy Mires, and crosses the North Teign and also a small tributary of that river on which Stone Tor Hill is placed. To this tributary the name of Wottes Brook is given, and a stream so called was the object which the perambulators of 1240 say formed the next bound to Thurlestone.

If this line is the correct one Watern Tor would fall some way within the Forest, and therefore could not have been the object to which the perambulators made their way on leaving Hound Tor. But as far as we know there is no return to any perambulation to be found among our public records that shews this line to be the true one; nor have we ever heard on the moor the name of Thurstone Tor given to Stone Tor Hill. Until we obtain confirmatory evidence on these points we shall prefer to believe that it was to the curiously-shaped rock at Watern Tor that the priours conducted the Sheriff and the company of knights on that July day nearly seven centuries ago.

Descending from the bold hill on which this tor rears its granite crest, the perambulators found themselves on the swampy flat between the Wallabrook and the North Teign, one part of which afterwards came to be known as

The confluence of the Wallabrook and the North Teign

Battery Meres. The stream to which the boundary line led them falls into the Teign, for so the Sheriff's return expressly states. The point which formed the Forest boundary was probably the confluence of the two streams; in fact, there can be little doubt about it, for the perambulation names the bound as being Wotesbrokelakesfote, that is, the foot of the Wotes Brook Lake, lake being a term applied on Dartmoor to minor streams. In 1609 the name had become changed to Whoode Lake, and this seems now to be lost; but that the 'lake' was the small affluent of the Teign which rises close to Stone Tor Hill we can hardly doubt.

From the point where Wottes Brook flows into the larger stream the line is drawn to Heighestone, by which name we shall have no difficulty in recognising the menhir, or high stone, which stands on the common not far from Kes Tor, in the neighbourhood of Chagford, and which still marks the Forest boundary.

This rude stone pillar belongs to an extensive group of pre-historic remains. The antiquary today finds much to interest him in the examination of the despoiled stone rows and circles and broken kists, but if he could see them as the Sheriff and his goodly company beheld them how greatly would that interest be increased. What were the ideas concerning these monuments of the men who viewed the bounds of the Earl of Cornwall's chase we know not. But we can at least be certain on one point. They shewed a far greater respect for them than have those who lived in more recent times. The vandals who have destroyed so many of the Dartmoor antiquities appeared upon the scene long after the knights of King Henry had turned to dust; the greater number, it is to be feared, did their work in the enlightened 19th century.

When, nearly 370 years later, the jury of survey passed this way on their journey round the Forest limits the work of spoliation had probably begun. A farm had been enclosed near by, and is incidentally mentioned by them, for they speak of the Menhir, or High Stone, as 'lyinge near ffernworthie hedges.' We may, therefore, well suppose that stones were taken from the rows and circles with which to build these.

Fernworthy, which is situated on the South Teign, just within the confines of the Forest, may possibly have been enclosed some considerable time before the survey of 1609, but it is not one of the ancient Forest farms. The probability is that it was not formed until long after Dartmoor ceased to be a Royal Forest. The present house, which there is little doubt is built on the site of the older one, appears to be of 17th century date.

When the perambulators had crossed the South Teign, and mounted the slope on its southern side, they were in sight of the head of the glen through which the river leaves the moor. In this hollow, below the farm of Thornworthy, and concealed by the trees, are some ruined walls, forming the remains of two huts of the tin streamers. Of these is related a variant of the story attaching to White Slade, in the valley of the East Dart, and which I have told in another place. This is not the only instance on Dartmoor of a tradition having two versions which are found widely apart.

According to the story the rude houses in this lonely glen were once the homes of two families. Where they came from nobody knew, nor who, or what they were; all that could be affirmed was that they were not Dartmoor people 'born and braid.' It did not appear from what the few dwellers in the neighbourhood could learn, that the families had been acquainted before they came to take up their abode there, nor did they then seem to become intimate, though living so near to each other. The head of one of these families was soon found to be a very industrious man, and when not at work for the farmers, would set off to the moor, cutting peat or ferns, in order to supply himself with fuel and his pig with bedding. It was needful that he should work hard, for besides his own and his wife's, he had half a dozen little mouths to fill. But with all his labour he could get barely sufficient to keep body and soul together. His features grew sharper, and his clothes seemed to grow larger, and his appearance altogether became painfully indicative of the usual state of his larder. His wife and his children were in no better condition than he, and certainly shewed that over-feeding was not one of their vices. Even the pig had to be content with half rations, but he made up for it by gorging himself when the acorns were on the ground.

A wide contrast to all this was afforded by the family of the poor man's neighbour. As for the man himself, beyond cutting a little peat occasionally, or a few ferns or rushes, he was never seen to do any work. He, too, had a wife and children, more children in fact than his neighbour, but they never looked as though they were hungry. On the contrary, they grew rosy cheeked and stout, and could not have presented a better appearance had they lived on the fat of the land. And it was on fat that they did live, but not, as those in the neighbourhood at first thought, on fat mutton. When the rotundity of person became noticeable in the man and the members of his family, and its was known that he did no work, it began to be hinted that those who had sheep pastured on the moor, had better look well after them. Animals were often missing. Might they not find their way to the house in the glen? It was resolved that when the loss of a sheep was next reported the neighbours would go thither in a body, and see whether such as the case.

An occasion soon arose for putting this resolve into execution. A fine sheep was missing from a flock pastured near the glen. The farmers who lived in the vicinity were hastily called together, and away they marched to the house of the family, the members of which, by their oily appearance and obeseness, had attracted so much notice. Entering the house the visitors searched high and low for the missing sheep, but there was no sign of it. Nor could a scrap of meat of any description be found; the larder of the thin and hungry-looking neighbour could not have been more ill-supplied. There was a mystery. On what did these people with the plump cheeks and dimpled chins live? The answer was soon forthcoming. One of the company had observed several blocks of granite placed in a row by the wall of the kitchen. These were partly covered with coarse towels, which he could not help thinking was very strange. Impelled by curiosity, he lifted one of the cloths, and the secret was revealed. The granite blocks had hollows cut in them, forming, as it were, small shallow troughs, and these were filled with black slugs. Great, plump, black slugs, preserved in salt; and on this greasy food the family subsisted. Should a doubt be cast upon this story, the visitor may see not only the ruins of the two houses, but also the blocks of granite with the hollows sunk in them, and which he will learn are usually regarded as sufficient proofs of its truth. Some may incline to think that the hollows are moulds into which the tinner poured the smelted ore, and were not made to contain salted slugs. But all are not sceptics.

The bond-mark towards which the perambulators made their way on leaving the South Teign was presumably a rude pillar, which they name Langestone, or, as another reading has it, Yessetone. This bound seems to be identical with one of later times known as Heath Stone, but it cannot be so regarded with certainty. In fact, the boundary line of the Forest for a distance of about 1¾ miles southward of the South Teign, is difficult to trace, as laid down by the perambulators of 1240. The bound succeeding Langestone is given as the turbary of Alberysheved, or Abereshеved, and the next one as the Wallabrook. Alberysheved, by which name is probably meant the head of some stream then known as the Alber, or Albery, cannot now be positively identified, nor can the stream referred to as the Wallabrook. The jury of 1609 identify the turbary of Alberysheved with a place at that time called Turf Hill, but as this name is now lost we are not helped much by them. They do not mention Wallabrook in connection with that spot, but from Turf Hill draw the line to a bond-mark, about the exact position of which we can fortunately be in no doubt.

The cairn on Water Hill, situated close to King's Oven

This is King's Oven, which is situated on the hill rising immediately behind a little hostelry known as the Warren House Inn, on the road between Princetown and Moretonhampstead, and about 7 miles from the former place. A short distance to the north-east a branch of the Bovey river rises, and there is some reason for supposing that it was this stream which the Sheriff alluded to in his return as the Wallabrook. If it were not it is difficult to see what other stream could be intended. The boundary line of this part of the Forest is usually drawn nearly straight from the South Teign to the point we have now reached.

King's Oven was probably an ancient smelting-place, and may have derived its name from the right of pre-emption of the tin raised in the Stannary of Devon, possessed by the King. Of the building which formerly existed on the hill only faint vestiges now remain. But when the Sheriff and the knights reached it on the evening of the day on which they set out from Cosdon they found within its walls a friendly shelter, for it was there, the tradition tells us, they rested when the sun went down.

Among the tributary streams of Dartmoor there are several bearing the name of Wallabrook, which it has been supposed they derive from the Celtic inhabitants of the moor, or Wealas, as they were termed by their Saxon conquerors. The word is the same as 'Welsh,' and signifies 'foreigner' or 'stranger,' and was used by the new settlers to indicate those who were not of their race. It was to the source of a stream of this name that the perambulators took their way when, after their night's sojourn at the furnace house of the tinners, they resumed their journey round the Forest. Whatever difference of opinion may exist respecting the boundary line of the latter between Cosdon and the King's Oven, there can be none about its course from the Oven onward for several miles. Men cannot well break the ancient law and remove a bond-mark when this happens to be a river, nor can it usually be argued that the same has found for itself a new channel. Consequently the Wallabrook having been fixed upon in the old days as a dividing line between the Forest and the commons, there has never been any dispute about the boundary in this quarter of the moor.

The Wallabrook rises near the Princetown and Moreton road, a short distance north-east of the Warren House Inn, and after a course of over 4 miles falls into the East Dart. But rivers form the boundary much further than this; indeed, with the exception of one break, and that not of great length, the Forest limits are defined by streams from the southern verge of Chagford Common to the northern border of Brent Moor, a distance of over 10 miles.

During their journey from Cosdon to the springs of the Wallabrook the perambulators had seen nothing within the Forest indicative of man's occupancy, but ere they had traced the stream very far, signs that he had pushed his way into this remote region became visible. Here, where the ground sloped gently from the bank towards the west were the enclosures of Walna, afterwards known as Warner, a farm of the early settlers on the moor, and further down another, named Runnage, with which the former is always associated in the Forest records.

Two and half centuries after the perambulators passed down this valley more land appears to have been added to these farms. In the forester's account for the year 1491 is an entry of '2d. of new rent of Richard Canna for a certain parcel of land lying between Stoddesbrook and Walbrook midstreme, so descending by les midstreme of the said water called Walbrook to the Churchway of the said Richard, leading from his tenement towards the Church of Widdicombe, so demised to the same Richard to hold to him and his heirs, according to the custom of the Forest.' Stoddesbrook, or, as it is now called, Statsbrook, rises in a miry spot to the eastward of Meripit Hill, and is crossed, almost at its source, by the Princetown highway about half a mile from the Warren House Inn. It falls into the Wallabrook a short distance above Runnage farmhouse, and in the angle formed by the two streams is the piece of land conveyed to Richard Canna over 400 years ago. The churchway alluded to is now a good road, and forms the most convenient means of reaching Widecombe from Post Bridge. It is carried over the Wallabrook by a clapper bridge, close to Runnage.

Not far below the latter farm the perambulators reached what was at that time probably the largest settlement in the Forest, or, at all events, shared that position with another. This was Pizwell, or, as we find it named in the Register of Bishop Bronescombe, Pushyll, the other being Babeney, anciently Balbenye. The entry is of the date 1260, 20 years after the perambulation of the Earl of Cornwall was made, and relates to the transfer for ecclesiastical purposes of the two 'villages' from the parish of Lydford to that of Widecombe.

Pizwell Farm and stepping stones

At the present day Pizwell retains more of a primitive air than any other cluster of ancient dwellings in the Forest. Less than a quarter of a century ago Hexworthy, another early settlement, also presented an old-time appearance, but of late years one or two modern erections have taken the place of older ones that had fallen to decay and have partly spoiled it from a picturesque point of view. But the three dwellings which constitute Pizwell are still much as of yore, and with their rough stone walls and roofs of thatch harmonise well with their solitary surroundings. This Forest settlement, which, as we know, has been the home of the moor farmer for about 700 years, and in all probability for a much longer period, may conveniently be reached from Post Bridge, from which place it is 1½ miles distant by road.

Making their way down the valley, and in sight of other farms, the Sheriff and his company at length reach Babeney, near the southern extremity of a ridge peninsulated by the stream they have been following, and the East Dart. Less than half a mile below this 'village' the knights arrive at the confluence and behold for the first time a branch of that river which gave name to the Forest they are perambulating. Thrown across the Wallabrook, and not far from where it mingles its waters with those of the Dart, the visitor may see today a very good example of a clapper bridge. Two rude piers stand in the stream, and with the abutments form three openings for the water. The stone laid across the central one is 9 feet 10 inches long; the two others are shorter. The total length of the bridge is about 23 feet, and its height at the centre about 5 feet. When the East Dart became the guide of the perambulators, they found themselves in a romantic valley with the peak of Yar Tor high above them on the left, and on the right a steep hillside, which some settlers had chosen as the site of their homesteads. This was the place which we now call Brimpts, a shortened form of its earlier name, and where, in 1307, Gregory de Bremstonte entered into the moiety of a tenement which his father held there. Oak trees were growing on the slope, for it is known that many were felled here a hundred years ago, sufficiently large for chip timber. Immediately below the spot where the dwellers in these more favoured of the Forest farms crossed the Dart, when they betook themselves to Widecombe, or its neighbourhood, the perambulators found that the river they had been following through the narrow valley was met by another. This was the West Dart. But we are not told whether the confluence of the two streams was then called by any distinguishing name. When, however, we do find such to be the case, we learn that it bore the same as it at present bears, the appropriate one of Dartmeet. This was in 1689, but how much earlier it was so called does not appear.

There are probably fewer places on Dartmoor better known to the visitor than Dartmeet. Beautifully placed, with romantic surroundings, and readily accessible by road, that the confluence of the two chief streams of the moorland region should become a favourite haunt with those who seek health or recreation there, is not to be wondered at. But the valley at Dartmeet does not convey a true idea of what Dartmoor really is; nor does the district through

The clapper at Dartmeet

which passes the road from Princetown thither. Although there is little cultivation, the enclosures seen throughout the way impart to the country a different aspect from that which it wears in those parts where Nature has hindered man's approach by making it abundantly clear to him that he could there only build his walls at a loss.

Passing up the West Dart the perambulators soon entered a part of the valley now known as Huccaby Cleave, or, as the moorman calls it, Huccaby Clay, and sometimes Clay Combe, it being too much trouble for him to sound the 'v'. Here some charming scenes of rock and river are presented, and it is scarcely a matter for surprise that tradition has made it a haunt of the pixies. Amid the wilderness of ferns and bushes and grey rocks are seen a few sycamores, and beneath these is the cave of the little elves. It is known as the Piskies' Holt, and forms a narrow subterranean passage, extending for a distance of 37 feet. But the pixies are never seen now, though they still live in the lore of the people of the moorland district.

The West Dart was not the companion of the perambulators for long. At Week Ford, a stream called in 1240 the Oke Brook, and in 1609 the Wo Brook, falls into it, coming from a valley on the south, and this forming here the Forest boundary, the Sheriff and his company take it as their guide. The name of this tributary stream, it is not unlikely, is derived from the Saxon 'wog,' meaning 'crooked,' a word descriptive of its course. Between Week Ford and Saddle Bridge, which is rather less than half a mile up the stream, are some charming little spots, such as the visitor would hardly suspect existed on Dartmoor. Mossy nooks, where ferns of a kind not usually met with on the moor are nodding in the spray of the falling waters, and half concealed by the graceful mountain ash. And these trees are seen growing further up the stream, where the moor assumes a sterner aspect, and their presence somewhat softens the wildness of the scene.

But this valley, so quiet and peaceful now, was once, tradition has it, a place to be shunned. It was the haunt of a dragon, a huge winged serpent, who preyed upon the flocks and herds of those who dwelt in the vicinity. One of its lurking-places may still be seen above the left bank of the Wo Brook. It is a hut circle, the walls of which are much higher than those usually found in erections of the kind. Here it was this dreadful monster was wont to lay in wait for his prey, and woe to the luckless wight who chanced to approach the spot, for so insatiable was the dragon's appetite that human beings or animals were alike acceptable to him; all were fish that came into his net. Dartmoor men are not made of the stuff that would tamely submit to oppression, and it was resolved that the terror of the neighbourhood should be got rid of. By what means the capture of the dragon was effected does not transpire, for, unfortunately, the tradition is altogether silent on the point. But that he was secured is certain, if the story is to be believed, and the Dartmoor men rid themselves of him in a very simple manner. They bound him 'hand an' voot, an' draw'd 'n in Dart.'

About a mile up the valley, and just where it bends towards the west, the perambulators reached the next bound, which we find from the Sheriff's return was then called Dryeworke. Early in the 17th century it also bore the name of Drylake, which it continues to do to this day, though it is generally referred to in the plural number. It is a shallow hollow, and as its early name and present appearance amply testify, has been the scene of the operations of the tinners. Forsaking the Wo Brook, the perambulators ascended this rocky hollow, and on reaching its head pursued a direction nearly due south to the next bound, which is scarcely 3/4 mile distant from the preceding one, if we take that to be, as it is probable we should, the lower end, or foot, of the hollow. This boundary the Sheriff returns as Dryfeld Ford, and it seems not to have lost that name some 400 years later, though at that time it also possessed another, the place being referred to in the survey of 1609 as 'Crefeild fford or Dryefeild ford.' It must not be supposed that the 'ford' has here a reference to a crossing-place over a stream. Crefield, or Corfield Ford, is on a hill over 1,500 feet in height, and is not near a river. The word is simply the Celtic 'ffordd', a way, or path, and its application in the present instance is, in all probability, to the old track known as Sandy Way, which passes close to the spot. The name by which the Sheriff of Devon knew this bond-mark of the Forest, in 1240—Dryfeld Ford, and which the perambulators of 1609 were also able to identify – is not now found in the locality in its old form though it exists there in another. The moormen speak of the spot as Filfer Head, and it is impossible to doubt that in the first part of this name we have the final syllables of the ancient appelation of the place.

From Crefield Ford the Forest boundary runs to Knattleborough, given variously on the copies of the Sheriff's return as Battyshull, Cattyshill, and

Gnattishull. Though still retaining the name of Knattleborough, the moormen always refer to it as Ryder, the 'borough' being an insignificant barrow, or cairn, on the summit of Ryder's Hill. On the mound are two bound stones, one serving to mark the limits of the common lands of Buckfastleigh and the other those of Holne, which here abut on the Forest.

If when the perambulators reached Knattleborough the conditions of the weather were favourable, they looked upon as extensive a prospect as it is possible to gain from any of the frontier heights of Dartmoor. Upon a clear day we have obtained from this spot, which attains an elevation of 1,692 feet, so wide a view that its extreme points embraced the Island of Portland, in Dorset, and the Lizard Point, in Cornwall. A short distance to the south-east of Knattleborough is another of the numerous Wallabrooks, though the first syllable of the name in this instance is usually softened, and it appears as Wellabrook. The prefix Wester is also given to it to distinguish it from the other streams similarly called. The Forest line runs direct from Knattleborough to the head of this stream, which then becomes the boundary throughout its course of about 1½ miles. Close to its source is a granite pillar marking the boundary of Buckfastleigh Moor, which is conterminous with the Forest from Knattleborough to a point nearly halfway down the stream. When the perambulators followed this stream to the Avon, into which river it falls, they probably saw, as we do now, that the tin-seeker had been busy on its banks, though it is at the same time certain that succeeding centuries witnessed much of what he has done there. But they did not see enclosures in the Forest here, for these are of comparatively recent dates, and pertain to Huntingdon Warren, which was not formed until early in the 19th century. In fact, the only enclosures to which the Sheriff and knights were near during their perambulation of the Forest were those which commenced at Walna, and ended at Hexworthy, near Week Ford. The rest of the circuit took them only through a wild district, into which the upland farmer had not intruded.

But the hill of Huntingdon, though enclosures do now exist there, cannot be greatly altered in aspect since the time when the knights looked upon it. With the exception of a wall, now in a ruinous condition, and which, in fact, was never completed, though it was probably intended to carry it round the whole of the ground included in the grant from the Duchy, the only signs of man's handiwork are a few small pasture crofts near a solitary warren house.

From the confluence of the Wellabrook and the Avon, or Aune, to give the latter stream its ancient name, the boundary line went straight to a huge cairn on the summit of a lofty hill to the south. This cairn is known as Eastern Whitaburrow (pronounced with the 'i' long), and was so called at the time the perambulation was made, the Sheriff recording the bound as Ester Whyteburghe. It is no less than 90 yards in circumference and 12 yards in height, and may be seen on the hill above the valley of the Avon from the little border town of South Brent. Eastern Whitaburrow marks the southernmost point of the Forest, but consequent upon an encroachment in this part of it, the

Eastern Whitaburrow

Western Whitaburrow

whole of the hill on which the cairn is situated is now claimed as belonging to Brent Moor. This we shall have occasion to notice later, but in passing may observe that in the perambulation of 1240, the survey of 1609, and another of the year 1786, Eastern Whitaburrow is named as a bond-mark of the Forest.

From this lofty burial place of a long-forgotten day the perambulators made their way towards the next bound, which is formed by the confluence of streams. But ere they have proceeded far they reach another cairn, not so large as the former, and which we now call Western Whitaburrow. From this point the Sheriff and the company which has journeyed with him can look far into the moorlands, and see many a tor lifting its head against the northern sky. The most distant hill is a rounded eminence, which is revealed through an opening cleft at some distant period by the waters of the Dart. The company do not know what hill it may be, but the priors tell them. It is Cosdon, the point whence they set out and soon their faces will be turned towards it, for they have half completed the circuit of the Forest.

There are not many places in England that present today quite the same appearance as they did in the 13th century. The scenes of historical events, even where they have been but little disturbed by the changes which time has wrought, wear an aspect not altogether like their earlier one. But the rambler in the south quarter of Dartmoor, who descends from Western Whitaburrow to Red Lake, as did the perambulators of the waste of Richard, Earl of Cornwall, sees only that which they saw in the summer of the year 1240. Not a single feature is changed. The slopes of Green Hill, prized by the moorman for the excellence of the pasturage, are now as they then were. No enclosures, no ruined walls; nothing to mar the work of Nature. The Erme, one of Dartmoor's most beautiful streams, rolls at the foot of the steep shoulder that forms the termination of Outer Stall Moor, and which is clothed in the mantle of heather it has worn for centuries.

We are not told in every one of the copies of the Sheriff's return to what part of Red Lake the perambulators made their way, but it would appear that they went direct to its confluence with the Erme. It is so stated in the survey of 1609, where the boundary line is said to run from Eastern Whitaburrow 'linial-lie to Redlake foote whir it falleth into Erme.' The last few words are, in a measure, unnecessary, but those who then viewed the limits of the Forest had a reason for being particularly explicit, for, as we shall see, the work of pushing out the bounds of the parish commons over the line of the Forest, had already begun. The perambulators tell us that from Red Lake the boundary was carried to Grymsgrove, but unfortunately it cannot now be determined with certainty what place was intended by that name. Those who viewed the bounds in 1609 considered it to be identical with Erme Head, and if the Erme marked the Forest limits, as they say it did, their supposition is probably correct. Erme Head is situated about midway between Red Lake Foot and Eylesbarrow, which latter is the bound named as succeeding Grymsgrove. There is a reason for believing that Erme Head once possessed some distinctive appellation. The miry spot that forms the source of the river is in the midst of ancient tin workings of considerable extent, and, like others, of an important character on the moor, these, in all probability, bore a name, which would attach itself to the locality. This seems to have been lost in 1609, but that the jury of survey had good reason for believing the place to be Grymsgrove we may be sure. In their presentment at the court held at Okehampton on 16th August in that year, they say that they found the bounds of the Forest of Dartmoor to be such as they then returned, partly upon the evidence afforded by copies of ancient records, partly upon that gleaned from individuals, and partly from their own knowledge, and that they were those which had been, and then were, recognised.

The modern suggestion that Grymsgrove means the grave of Grim, and that it is represented by a kistvaen on the bank of a feeder of the Plym, is ingenious, but that is all. And even supposing such really were the meaning of the name, it might quite as well belong to another kist, which is much nearer to the recognised Forest line. Unless we are to suppose that the jury of survey who were chosen to view the bounds in 1609 were totally unfit for the task, there appears to be no sufficient reason for casting doubts upon what they tell us. Since they passed over the ground there has been no question on the moor as to the correctness of their return of the boundary between Red Lake Foot and Erme Head, and the latter is regarded as Grymsgrove.

From Erme Head the perambulators passed up the slope to the west, and on gaining the summit of the ridge many of the hills on the western border of the moor came suddenly into view. Sheeps Tor rises boldly against the sky, with Lether Tor and Sharp Tor, and where the hills recede the eye looks through the opening upon a wide prospect of woods and fields, bounded by the Cornish Hills. Close to where they stand is a rock, barely a dozen feet in length, and about three in height, and with a fairly level surface. It is not named as a Forest bond-mark, but it is on the boundary line. It is now known as Broad Rock, and this name is inscribed upon it, and also the letters B.B. The latter stand for

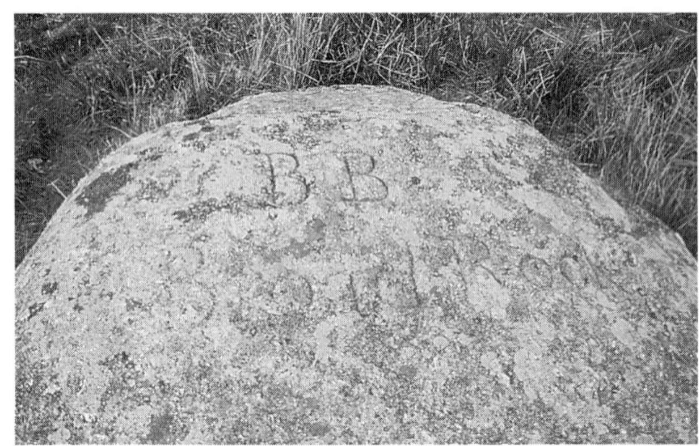

Broad Rock

Blatchford Boundary, the rock serving to mark the limits of that manor. We recollect when a pole was fixed by the side of Broad Rock, and it formed a very useful mark to those journeying between Princetown and Ivybridge or Brent. It disappeared, however, nearly 30 years ago. From Broad Rock the perambulators descended to the Plym, which they crossed not far below its source, and made their way to Elysburghe, and which place we can readily identify, the form of the name having changed but little. But the jury of 1609 named the Plym as a bound. They draw the line from Grymsgrove to Plym Head, by which we can only imagine that they meant the upper waters of that stream, and not its actual source, which certainly lies some way within the Forest. Other districts on the moor near the springs of rivers are similarly called. Thus, when Walkham Head is spoken of the ground around the upper part of the Walkham Valley is meant, and not the exact spot where the water oozes from the mire. The Walkham Head Peat Works, now deserted and fallen to decay, were situated at some little distance below where the river takes its rise, and the same may be said of the Rattle Brook Head Peat Works. But Plym Head was the name recorded by the jurors, and as a consequence the bounds of the common land belonging to the parish of Shaugh have been pushed out to that point. But there can be no doubt whatever that the true line is from Erme Head, or Grymsgrove as it may be termed, direct to Eylesbarrow. Two dilapidated barrows placed on the summit of the hill mark the boundary at the latter spot. Thence the line runs to Siward's Cross, one of the most interesting of the medieval monuments in the Forest, and which, according to tradition, owes its name to the great Earl of Northumberland, who is said to have owned lands in this quarter of the moor in the time of the Confessor. When we come to trace the boundaries of certain manors which were bestowed upon one of the great monastic houses of Devonshire, we shall find that Siward's Cross is named as a bond-mark. As an opportunity will then be afforded us of examining it, we

Eylesbarrow Cairn, surrounded by winter snow

The Perambulation of Dartmoor Forest, July 24, 1240: the twelve knights and their retainers at Nun's (or Siward's) Cross.

South Hisworthy (Look Out) Tor

shall not linger by it now, but hasten onward with the Sheriff and his company, for there is much ground to be traversed ere we complete the circuit of the Forest.

A bank of stone and turf, or, as such are termed on Dartmoor, a reave, now marks the Forest line in this part of its course, and leads towards the enclosures of Tor Royal, where the next bound comes in sight. This is a pile of rocks which the perambulators tell us was known as Ysfother, but which we now call Hisworthy, or, as the name is usually pronounced, Hessary. To distinguish it from another tor of the same name to which the boundary line runs direct it bears the prefix of South, but in the locality is seldom called by any other name than Look Out Tor. South Hisworthy Tor is less than a mile from Princetown, and is approached by a good path, that part of it nearest the moorland capital being known as Ivybridge Lane. This name it obtained many years ago, when it was customary to escort released prisoners from the convict depot, across the moor to Ivybridge, where they were entrained. The route led by South Hisworthy Tor, and from thence to Broad Rock was very nearly on the line of the Forest boundary.

The visitor approaching Princetown by the high-road from Dousland will observe on the outskirts, and on the right of the road, a granite post. This is one of several bond-stones placed between South Hisworthy and North Hisworthy Tors, and beyond the latter, to mark, like the reave near Siward's Cross, the line between the Common of Walkhampton and the Forest. Another stands close to Princetown Station, and it is not until the train passes this mark that the traveller to that place finds himself in the ancient hunting-ground of the Norman Sovereigns. Up to this point his moorland journey has been only within its purlieus.

North Hisworthy crowns the lofty hill which rises like a huge barrier between the prison and the open country to the westward. The perambulators of 1240 speak of it as 'another' Ysfother; there is no distinguishing name. The jurors of 1609 refer to the southern pile as Little Hisworthie, but mention the northern without a prefix. Ninety years later we find the tors distinguished as at the present day. This is in a deposition taken in a suit for tithes, in 1699, the plaintiff being David Birchincha, rector of Lydford. The deponent was Quintin Brown, a yeoman of Holne, and in naming the bounds of a portion of Lydford parish he mentions South Hessworthy and North Hessworthy. Here we not only find the prefixes as now employed, but also the form of the name. It is scarcely necessary to explain that in the speech of the inhabitant of the moor the termination 'worthy' would be considerably shortened, and thus the name would be sounded Hessary. Many other Dartmoor place-names that have changed in a similar manner might be mentioned, among them Hexworthy, which the surveyors of the early part of the 19th century, misled by the local pronunciation, have set down on their map as Haxary.

In passing through this part of the moor the perambulators looked upon a very different scene from that which meets the eye of the observer today. As the Sheriff of Devon, and the knights, and the priours, and the ever-increasing throng, mounted the slope of Hisworthy, a wide view of the Forest unfolded itself, but throughout the whole of its visible extent they saw nothing beyond, perhaps, one or two thatched roofs, to tell them that man shared the possession of that lonely land with the wolf and the deer. But now, though he may look into parts of the moor as wild as they were of old, the district that stretches away towards the east from the foot of Hisworthy has lost much of its primeval appearance. Numerous enclosing walls are seen, weathered and grey, and though the face of the country shows no trace of the plough, one cannot but realise that Nature has been partly subdued. Where men once hunted the lordly stag his descendants have hunted for gold. It is probable that the earlier adventurers met with the most success.

But it is immediately below this lofty hill where the greatest change has taken place. Here is now a little town, with a railway station, and the great prison, with its gardens and pastures surrounding it. And the transformation has taken place in very recent times. For five and half centuries after the perambulators saw it in the days of Henry III the face of the moor was not altered. There is nothing attractive in North Hisworthy Tor itself, the pile being small and presenting no features of interest, but the view commanded from it is a wonderful one, and should on no account be missed by the visitor to Princetown. On one side a vast extent of moor, and on the other a range of country in which wood and water, rich pasturage and park-like slopes, towns and villages, go to make up a picture almost as varied as it is possible to conceive.

The perambulators mention no bound between North Hisworthy and Mis

Tor, neither does any occur in the later surveys, but in recent times the Forest line was, nevertheless, marked at about midway between those two points by a granite pillar. This was called the Rundle Stone, and is named in 1702 as marking the limits of the Forest, by a deponent in a suit similar to that in which Quintin Brown was concerned. It is also shown on a map published in 1720, where it is described as a 'Great stone call'd Roundle.' It stood very near where the road to Princetown branches from that running from Tavistock to Two Bridges, and its chief purpose was probably to mark an old track across the Forest. A few years ago this stone was broken up and used as material for a wall belonging to the prison enclosures. This was done presumably by convicts, who having broken the laws of their country were set by those in whose charge they were to break up one of its antiquities. Upon whom should rest the blame for such an act of vandalism we have not discovered.

Fortunately, we are able to give some particulars of this stone, having taken measurements of it about 20 years ago, when it was standing by the roadside. It was a rough pillar 4 feet in girth, and 7 feet in height above the few stones with which it was wedged in the ground. Near the top was the letter 'R' 7 inches high, and carved in relief. Afterwards we saw it serving as a gate-post close by, and still later it lay upon the ground immediately within the enclosure. Now all that remains of it is its name, the locality being still known as Rundle Stone.

The Sheriff of Devon has left it on record that from Hisworthy his company of knights passed onward by the middle of Mis Tor, which has been supposed to mean that they made their way through the midst of Mis Tor Moor to the tor itself. That the latter, or at all events one of the piles of which it consists, was the recognised bond-mark, there is evidence in a deed 40 years later date to show, and this we shall by-and-bye notice. The formation of the tor is such that the line could have been drawn between its several piles, and thus have gone 'per mediam Mystor,' as the perambulators say it did. But unless a particular pile marked the line we cannot suppose this to have been the case, for according to the Forest Law an object serving as a bound of a Forest was deemed to be wholly within its limits. However this may have been, there is certainly reason for believing that a particular rock was fixed upon to mark the line. This has on its surface a circular hollow about 3 feet in diameter and 7 or 8 inches in depth, which is still known by the name it bore in the 13th century. Mis Tor Pan, as it is called, was long regarded as being an artificial cavity, and as a matter of course its formation was ascribed to the Druids. But it is now known that the wind and the rain and the frost scooped out this and similar hollows on the rocks of Dartmoor. It is pleasant to think that the Druids, if there ever were any in the land of tors, had something better to do than waste their time in making granite basins. But if science has banished the Druids from Mis Tor, it has not succeeded in ridding it of its traditional association with the Evil One. The hollow in the rock has been said to be the work of Satan, and was made by him to serve as a cooking utensil. Hence it is sometimes referred to as the

Devil's Frying-pan.

Although the common over which the perambulators passed as they approached this tor is not now known as Mis Tor Moor, there is nothing unreasonable in supposing that it bore that name in 1240. The jurors of 1609 speak of it as such, stating that the Forest line ran 'through the midst of Mistorr Moore to a rocke called Mistorpann.' Later on the name appears to have fallen into disuse, not being mentioned in the presentment of a jury who made a survey in 1786, and who trace the boundary 'to North Hisworthy, thence to Mistor Pan.'

Descending the steep side of Mis Tor, the perambulators crossed the Walkham, and made their way to the summit of the ridge which runs parallel to the upper waters of that stream, and rises above its right bank. From the river they probably passed up the little coombe, where rises a spring known as Dead Lake Well, and which the whortleberry pickers will tell the visitor is deliciously cool even on the hottest summer day. Dead Lake is not mentioned by the Sheriff, the bound following Mis Tor being entered on the return to the writ as Mewyburghe, but the later surveys name it. The jurors of 1609 draw the line from Mis Tor Pan to Dead Lake Head, and say they consider the latter to be the Mewyburghe of 1240. By this they probably meant the large barrow to the north of Dead Lake Head, and to this bond-mark there is no doubt the earlier perambulators directed their steps in crossing the Walkham. The boundary line here pursues a course nearly due north to the Tavy, being conterminous with that of the extensive commons included in the hamlet of Willsworthy, one of the ancient vils, or early settled places, bordering the Forest. The name by which the tumulus in which we see the Mewyburghe of other days is now known as Whitaburrow. Besides being a Forest bond-mark, it served to assure the traveller who had left the in-grounds for the heart of the moor that he was pursuing the track he should follow to reach the ford over the Walkham. The old path runs very near to the barrow, and is probably much more plainly defined now than in earlier days; having in recent times been considerably worn by the wheels of peat carts.

From Whitaburrow the boundary proceeds to Lynch Tor, named by the perambulators Lullingesfote, and by the jurors of 1609, Luntesborowe. The 'borowe' or cairn, is still to be seen there. The tor consists of two piles, neither of them of large size, one placed on the crest of the ridge, and the other a little below it on the slope to the west. The cairn is built round the higher pile, which not only its 17th century name, but its position, tells us is the one that was regarded as the bond-mark. Quite close to the pile are the walls of a hut of the description of those formerly erected by herdsmen, who were wont to gather their beasts at the tors.

Still proceeding northwards, the perambulators reach a small tributary of the Tavy, which we now call Wester, or Homer, Red Lake. Homer is used by the moorman in contradiction to 'outer', and signifies that the object to the name of which the term is prefixed is situated on the border side of another similarly

The cairn on Lynch Tor

called, or, in other words, that it is nearer home. Following the Red Lake to its confluence with the Tavy, the perambulators then took the latter stream for their guide, tracing it downward for a short distance to the point where it is joined by the Rattle Brook, at the head of Tavy Cleave. This confluence forms the next bound to Lynch Tor, and is set down in the Sheriff's return as Rakernesbrokysfote, that is the foot of the Rakern's Brook. This considerable tributary of the Tavy rises not far from Hunt Tor, or Hunter, as the moormen term it, and has a course of nearly 3 miles, running almost due south. It forms the boundary of the Forest throughout its length, and is the only object acting as such which has parts of the same parish on each side of it. The boundary line is drawn between the parish of Lydford, in which the Forest lies, and the commons belonging to the parishes surrounding it, consequently Lydford is always on one side of it, and a border parish on the other. But Lydford has also a common abutting on the Forest in precisely the same manner as the other parishes, and this it does in the valley of the Rattle Brook. When the stream, therefore, a short distance from its source, reaches the point where Lydford Common begins, it enters that parish, only leaving it a little before it mingles its waters with those of the Tavy.

Westward of the Rattle Brook, and rising from its bank, is Amicombe Hill, the scene of the Devil's banishment, when he was expelled from Widecombe-in-the-Moor. That place has sometimes been styled 'Widecombe-in-the-Cold Country', and how it came about that an individual accustomed to a particular warm clime, chose it for his abode is difficult to understand, but that he lived 'to Widecombe' was at one time confidently asserted. He was in evidence there on the day the church was damaged by the fearful thunderstorm, and was seen shortly before its occurrence by the landlady at Pound's Gate, who not only observed his cloven foot, but heard the liquor with which she served him run hissing down his throat, and afterwards found that the money she had taken in payment had changed to dried leaves. Cold Country or not, everybody knew that the Devil was never very far from Widecombe.

But the good folks of that secluded village came to the conclusion that his room would be far more desirable than his company, and by common consent he was banished to Amicombe Hill. It is unfortunate that he was not sent to a greater distance. The Devil had been able to endure the cold of Widecombe, but he could not stand the severe climate of Amicombe Hill. A wilder and more inhospitable spot it is perhaps impossible to find, and he whose natural element resembled Vesuvius felt that it was totally unsuited to him. He shrieked with rage when the icy winds chilled him to the bone, and often when the night is dark and the blast sweeps over the hill his howlings may be heard. It is difficult to reconcile this story with the too apparent fact that he is still at work in other places, but if it be not believed the visit to the hill on a stormy winter's night will be quite sufficient to convince the most sceptical that, if the unearthly sounds are a proof of it, the Devil is most certainly on Amicombe.

High Willes

From Rattle Brook Head the boundary goes to Stinka Tor, which is not far off, and thence to the West Ockment River. The perambulators trace it from the Rattle Brook to La Westsolle, but whether in this latter name we see that of the stream cannot with certainty be determined, but such is by no means improbable. The next bound is given as Ernestorre, which it is also difficult to identify. That this object is represented either by a pile of rocks now known as Foresland Ledge, or by the lofty summit of High Willes is very likely. There can be little doubt that the line ran from the West Ockment to High Willes, thence to Row Tor, and from there to the ford to the east of St. Michael's Chapel of Halstock. The boundary as claimed by the Okehampton commoners lies outside this line. The absence of a bound between Ernestorre, even if we could decide where that point was, and the ford near the chapel, in the return made by the knights in 1204, renders it difficult to trace the line. The only thing that is certain is that the commons have here been extended into the Forest. The boundary of the former is now said to run from Sandy Ford on the West Ockment, to Crovener Steps, a crossing-place on the East Ockment. This line seems to have been fixed upon by supposing the last-named ford to be that mentioned by the perambulators, which it most certainly is not. We shall have to refer to this boundary later.

Following in the footsteps of the Sheriff and his company, we make our way from High Willes to Row Tor, and thence by the Chapel of Halstock, of which little now remains but the name, to a fording-place over the East Ockment in the valley below. There is ample evidence to show that this line is the correct one. Even now, although it is claimed that the bounds of Okehampton Commons extend to Crovener Steps, there is a piece of land between them and the in-country which is still regarded in the locality as being part of the Forest. The crossing-place on the stream which we have now reached, and where there are stepping-stones, was used by those who were wont to betake themselves from the Belstone side of the valley to the little sanctuary above, and still bears the name of Chapel Ford.

Passing up the valley of the Ockment the perambulators mount the high ridge on the east, where the Belstone tors lift their rugged forms. Then is seen once more the valley of the Taw and the great sweep of Cosdon, whence they had set out on their journey. As they crossed the river where it leaves the wide plain stretching from the foot of Steeperton, we can well imagine that the day was drawing towards its close. The rocks on the crest of the ridge are gilded by the rays of the setting sun, but the side of the valley beneath the tors is in shadow, and the heather there has assumed a darker hue. They reach the bond-mark that had been their starting place, and their perambulation of the Forest is completed. The twelve knights summoned to view the bounds and the four who acted on behalf of the manorial lords are satisfied that they have been set down correctly, and the Sheriff of Devon is able to record that on the Eve of St. James the Apostle, 1240, the bounds of the great chase of Richard, Earl of Cornwall, have been perambulated obediently to the writ of the King.

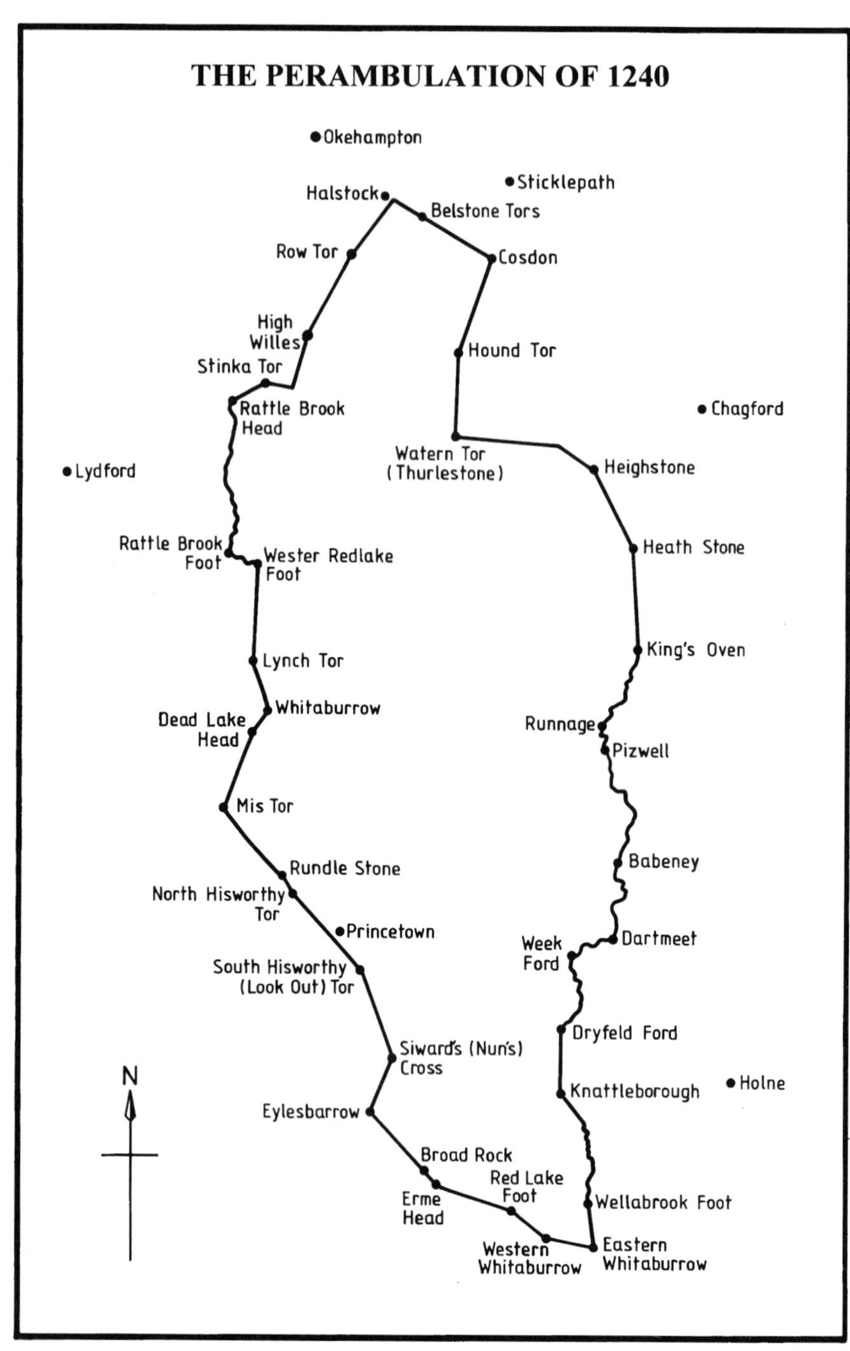

THE PERAMBULATION OF 1240
Okehampton
Sticklepath
Halstock
Belstone Tors
Row Tor
Cosdon
High Willes
Hound Tor
Stinka Tor
Rattle Brook Head
Chagford
Lydford
Watern Tor (Thurlestone)
Heighstone
Rattle Brook Foot
Wester Redlake Foot
Heath Stone
Lynch Tor
King's Oven
Whitaburrow
Dead Lake Head
Runnage
Pizwell
Mis Tor
Babeney
Rundle Stone
North Hisworthy Tor
Princetown
Week Ford
Dartmeet
South Hisworthy (Look Out) Tor
Dryfeld Ford
Siward's (Nun's) Cross
N
Knattleborough
Holne
Eylesbarrow
Broad Rock
Red Lake Foot
Erme Head
Wellabrook Foot
Western Whitaburrow
Eastern Whitaburrow

III

THE COMMONS OF DEVONSHIRE

The Forest of Dartmoor as defined by the metes and bounds alluded to in the Charter of King John and which have not since been materially altered, occupies considerably less than one-half of the moor. When mention of it first occurs we find it to be encircled, as it still is, by a broad belt of waste land belonging to the manors surrounding the moorland region. But though this waste was then and at a much earlier time, in the hands of different manorial lords, that it was once Royal demesne, like the Forest itself, there is not much doubt. Positive proof may be wanting, but more than one circumstance points to such a conclusion. To encroachments upon the Crown lands we may probably trace the origin of these extensive border commons. Those who dwelt upon the verge of the waste would pasture their flocks and herds upon it, and would supply themselves with peat for fuel, and with such other necessaries as the land afforded. After a long period of non-interference not only would common rights become established, but in the probable absence of well-defined boundaries, that part of the moor contiguous to the cultivated lands would be looked upon as waste of the manor in which they lay. At length would come a time when recognition of the bounds would be insisted upon, and we can conceive that the rights which long-usage had conferred would not be ignored. Then the boundary line of the King's demesne was so adjusted, that between it and the in-grounds there should be a sufficiency of common for each manor.

But the rights possessed by the Monarch over these commons were not relinquished with the ownership of them. These he still exercised, and his successors have done the same. The right of searching them for estrays, though sometimes disputed, the lord of the Forest of Dartmoor still possesses, and its existence forms a strong piece of evidence that the border commons were once Royal demesne. At what period these bounds of the King's lands were first fixed upon, it is, of course, impossible to say, but there is reason to believe that they were recognised in the time of the Confessor. When, therefore, William the Conqueror reserved for himself the lands he found vested in the Crown, the probability is that he became possessor of Dartmoor, but it would be only of that part of it lying within the ancient boundaries. The great tract of waste outside these came into the hands of those of his followers upon whom he bestowed the numerous manors bordering the moor.

In the time of Henry I, the bounds of his Dartmoor possessions did not form the bounds of his Forest. That certainly included within its ambit the whole of the Dartmoor region. This monarch afforested enormous tracts of land throughout the country, of which there is particular mention in the Charter of the Forest of 1224, the ninth of Henry III. It directs that the Forests of England shall be perambulated, and one of the clauses runs as follows: 'All Forests which King Henry our grandfather afforested and made shall be viewed by good and lawful men, and if he hath made Forest of any other wood, more than of his own demesne, whereby the owner of the wood hath hurt, we will that forthwith it be disafforested, saving the common of herbage and of other things in the same Forest to them which before were accustomed to have the same.' That the commons lying round the Royal demesne formed part of the land in Devonshire which had been 'made Forest,' and which the Charter of John, supplemented by the one cited, disafforested, we may be certain. When thus thrown out of the Forest they were considered as purlieus, a word derived from the French, and signifying a space immediately surrounding a Forest, but being exempt from its jurisdiction.

The holders of the border commons are referred to in the writ of Henry III, directing a perambulation of the Forest to be made, as we have seen, and in other documents several of these are named. We find that some of the commons were appurtenant to religious houses situated near their borders, and according to the statement made by certain jurors in 1275, one of these foundations seems to have claimed rights that did not belong to it. The jurors in question were those who made the return for the Hundred of Stanborough to the Royal Commission of Enquiry concerning encroachments on the rights of the King, called the Hundred Rolls. They say that in Henry III's time Howald, the Abbot of Buckfast, appropriated to his abbey a large tract of land in the south part of Dartmoor. He does not appear to have been interfered with, for, at the time of making their return, the jurors say that his successors were enjoying the land, and making profit by selling peat for fuel and letting out pasturage, to the injury of others, and by what right the jurors did not know. It is not stated whether this tract of land was situated within the Forest, or whether it comprehended only the two commons of Holne and Buckfastleigh, the manorial rights over which the abbey possessed. The first-named common was given to the abbey by Richard Bauzan, for the souls of his father and mother, and his brother Stephen Bauzan, as appears from a Charter Roll of the forty-third of Henry III. The donor bestowed upon the abbey all his land of Holne, with its appurtenances, among which are mentioned wastes, turbaries, and feedings, the charter being witnessed by Gilbert de Umframvile and others, and confirmed by the King.

But whether the abbots claimed exclusive rights over their two commons of Holne and Buckfastleigh, or over a part of the Forest itself, they most certainly could not have possessed such, though there may have been some grounds for causing them to imagine that they did. Richard I appears to have granted them certain liberties and free customs, which are alluded to in an undated charter, by which the Abbot of Buckfast relinquished his right to have a stud farm in the Forest to Richard, Earl of Cornwall. This was one of the privileges that had been granted by the Lion Heart, but all the others were to continue in force. It is possible that Howald, the Abbot, put his own construction upon the terms of the charter, and claimed more for the abbey than it had been intended he should.

The manor of Brent was also among the possessions of Buckfast Abbey, and included in this was the extensive common known as Brent Moor. Between the latter and the common lands of Buckfastleigh is Dean Moor, which did not belong to the abbey, but running from the in-ground of the Forest cut the moorland possessions of Buckfast into two parts. But Dean Moor was, nevertheless, in the hands of the monks. It belonged to Plympton Priory, so that the two houses shared between them the whole of the border commons of Dartmoor, extending from the Dart to the Glaze, adjoining the parish of Ugborough. The manor of Shaugh, which includes a considerable area of the common land within its bounds, was also among the possessions of Plympton Priory, and the vast tract comprising the commons of Walkhampton and Sheepstor formed part of the lands bestowed upon Buckland Abbey at its foundation.

Okehampton, which became the head of one of the great baronies that were created in Devonshire, was bestowed by the Conqueror on Baldwin de Brionys, to whom it is usual to attribute the building of Okehampton Castle. In this barony was included an extensive chase, which comprised within its boundaries the whole of the Okehampton Commons. Another holder of a tract of moorland was Richard de Redvers, to whom Henry I gave the Barony of Plympton, and who was created Earl of Devon by the same monarch. His descendant, Baldwin de Redvers, in the 13th century, granted to the burgesses of Plympton common of turbary for all necessary fuel for their houses in his moor 'towards Dartmoor,' that is to say on his commons, which lay between the cultivated lands of Plympton and the Royal Forest. This grant was confirmed by his daughter, Isabella de Fortibus. The manor of Gidleigh belonged to the family of Prouz, or Prous, from the time of the Conqueror until that of Edward II. They had a castle there, the picturesque remains of which may still be seen near the church, and an extensive park, or chase, on the verge of the moor. It extends for some distance along the left bank of the North Teign, which here flows through a deep and narrow valley, the sides of which are covered with trees, amid which are seen numerous masses of rock. Gidleigh Common lies between the wastes belonging to Throwleigh and Chagford, and was of more than ordinary importance, having on its verge one of the pounds to which estrays found on the Forest were driven.

In the first part of the 14th century the manors of Gidleigh and Throwleigh, the two commons belonging to which adjoin, were in the possession of John de

Alneto, as also was the manor of Cornwood, which is in quite another part of the moor. Other important manors having parts of the moorland within their boundaries were Cudlipp Town, near Peter Tavy; Spitchwick and Natsworthy, in Widecombe parish; Ugborough, on the southern borders of the moor; and Ermington, the tenants of which manor have rights of pasture on the long, narrow strip of waste lying along the left bank of the River Erme, and known as Harford Moor. In many of the border hamlets of Dartmoor may still be seen, often in a ruinous condition, the small manor pounds. Some are built with a due regard to regularity of form, as at Cudlipp Town and Pound's Gate, where they are square, and at Belstone, where the pound is circular in shape. At Gidleigh less care was taken, two walls enclosing a corner by the roadside being deemed sufficient, but as though to compensate for this obvious makeshift, the pound is not only furnished with an iron gate, but the latter also bears a legend informing the passer-by where the pound-keeper may be found.

The remains of the ruined castle at Gidleigh

As Gidleigh consists only of the ruined castle, the manor house, two cottages, and a modern dwelling, the necessity for this information is not obvious. In the hamlet of Willsworthy the now long-disused pound is formed of rough granite blocks, untouched by the tool, in the same manner as the walls of ancient enclosures on the moor are built. There are many others which the wanderer in the settlements on the fringe of Dartmoor will find for himself, and they form not the least interesting among the objects he will meet with, for they contribute something to the story of moorland border life.

There is more than one instance of a Dartmoor common thrusting itself, as it were, within what would appear to be the natural bounds of an adjoining one. Sampford Spiney does this, running up into the common lands of the parish of Whitchurch, in a long, narrow strip, and expanding at the end into a form closely approaching that of a lozenge in heraldry, or, as it is usually spoken of in the locality, the ace of diamonds on the cards. The story related in many parts of England in explanation of similar instances of small portions of a parish intruding upon another is found attached to two of the Dartmoor commons, Okehampton and Ugborough. It is to the effect that a stranger, a man whom nobody owned, was found dead on the moor, and those in whose parish the body lay refused to remove it and give it burial. Fortunately for the credit of humanity, so bad an example was not followed by the people of the adjoining parish. They laid the stranger in their churchyard, and then, reasoning that as they had been at some trouble and expense for the dead, it was only right that the living should benefit, they claimed that part of the common in which the body had been discovered. In the case of the two moors named, Okehampton intrudes itself upon Sourton, at a placed called Vellake Corner, and Ugborough thrusts itself into the Brent boundary at the Glazes, as the springs of the two branches of the Glaze Brook are called.

The perambulations of the border commons of the moor are usually made, if not with ceremony, at least with a due observance of old customs. At Okehampton the occasion of viewing the bounds is known as Spurling-day, and a great number of commoners and townspeople take part in the proceedings. It has been suggested that the term is a corruption of the word 'purlieu,' which is not unlikely, and it has been long in use. It does not, however, occur in the entry in the journal kept by Richard Shebbeare, of Okehampton, who filled the Mayoralty chair of that borough more than once. Under date 13th May, 1672, he says 'This day Mr. Mayor, with many of the inhabitants of this town, together with Mr. Hussey and Mr. Randall, schoolmaster, and divers both young and old, viewed the bounds of Dartmoor Commons, belonging to this parish.' At the present day the parishioners set out from the town, sometimes headed by a band of music, and make their way to the commons, and commence their perambulation at a point called Symons' Ditch. Thence proceeding to the easternmost boundary, they turn and make their way over the long range of commons towards the West Ockment. As the many miry places are passed on the way, apples and nuts are thrown into them, for which there is a scramble by the younger among those present. On reaching the slope below Yes Tor refreshments are generally partaken of, and with this pleasant break in the day's proceedings the bound-viewing, with a great many terminates. The attractions afforded by a descent into the valley of the West Ockment to Vellake Corner, and a climb up the hill towards Iron Gates, to say nothing of a probable sousing when crossing the river, are not sufficient to allure them from the creature comforts so temptingly spread before them on the turf.

In the adjoining parish of Belstone the commoners are equally alive to the importance of looking after the inner man en route, which they do at a bondstone at Taw Marsh, but they also believe in giving him a good start. Consequently before setting out, refreshments are served on the village green, and everyone is well braced for the task before him. Since it would by no means do to have all the feasting in the earlier stages of the proceedings, the bound-viewing is appropriately ended with a dinner. As Belstone is one of the smallest of the Dartmoor commons, the distance traversed is not very great, and it is therefore evident that the intervals between meals are not uncomfortably long, and that however keen the moorland air, one would be very unlikely to sink into that famished condition, sometimes experienced by the upland wanderer.

Among the customs observed in this perambulation is the carrying of a red flag by one of the party. Whether this is to be regarded as a danger signal, and is intended as a warning to those who may have over-braced themselves at starting, we are not in a position to say. A contrast is afforded by the two parishes of Belstone and South Tawton, which are adjacent. We do not mean in the matter of supplying themselves with refreshment on the occasions of viewing the bounds of their common. That pleasant custom is certainly not neglected by South Tawton; nor, indeed, do any of the Dartmoor parishes fail to recognise its necessity. But there is a great difference in the view which the man of Belstone takes of his common rights, and that with which the South Tawton men regard theirs. The former, who has been the most tenacious of his rights of any of the Devonshire commoners, looks upon his common purely as such – a place to be kept as it always has been, and which shall be of value to each parishioner, not only as a grazing ground, but in other ways, as yielding much that will 'do him good.' The South Tawton parishioner, on the contrary, considers his common as belonging to him so literally that he does not scruple to enclose portions of it as he feels inclined. In this parish the common is slowly, but surely, being taken from the goose. The Gidleigh parishioners, when they reach the menhir near Kes Tor have a custom somewhat similar to that of the Belstone men at Taw Marsh. We are not now alluding to the commissariat. The latter set one of the party, generally a boy, to stand upon his head on the bond-stone by which they halt. The Gidleigh commoners do not consider they have faithfully observed the old traditions until a boy has been made to climb the menhir, and stand upon its wedge-like summit, for the accomplishing of which feat he is rewarded with a sixpenny piece.

In viewing the bounds of Brent Moor the Avon has to be crossed, and here some of the party never fail to acquaint themselves with the temperature of a Dartmoor stream. As in other parts of the moor, when rivers are crossed at the time of bound-viewing, each of the party is supposed to possess the privilege of trying to thrust his neighbour into the stream, and a good deal of horse-play often takes place in consequence. This observance is particularly prominent in the perambulation of Harford Moor, when certain fishery rights connected with the manor of Ermington are duly exercised, the perambulators being more than once in proximity to the River Erme.

Though many of the customs observed at the time of viewing the bounds of parishes now take the form of practical jokes, and are seemingly meaningless, they are not in reality so, although their import is not always understood. In early times it was customary for every part of a boundary to be perambulated, and not, as at present, merely looked at where the ground presents difficulties.

While the line would not be likely to be drawn through places absolutely impassable, there might yet be many miry spots in its course, and these would have to be crossed. The inducing of boys to make their way into them is therefore only a survival of the custom once considered necessary, and so in the same manner is the throwing of persons into the streams when crossing them. The boundary line was supposed to be faithfully followed, and no considerations of personal comfort were allowed to interfere with the practice. The bounds of each of the Dartmoor commons are conterminous with those of two other commons, one being on either side, and the Forest. The former are adjusted between themselves; the latter, though it is not always admitted, is settled by the Forest boundary. When mistakes in fixing bond-stones between the commons occur it is generally found that the advantage has lain with the parish which has erected them. A case of this sort has occurred during the past summer on Black Down where the hamlet of Willsworthy is contiguous to the parish of Mary Tavy. Bond-stones were set up by the former, but instead of being placed on the recognised boundary line they were fixed some yards outside it. The parish boundary, which is conterminous with that of the Forest, may, speaking generally, be looked upon as running in the line which the Forest perambulators and jurors of survey have described in their returns, parish bound-viewing notwithstanding. Though we do not possess a return to any perambulation of the Forest made between 1240 and 1609, yet it must not be forgotten that during the period which elapsed between those dates, the Forest was carefully looked after by the reeves, the foresters, and the priours, and its boundaries must have been well known to them. Any attempt to thrust back these bounds would at once have been prevented. The commoners might claim, and probably did, portions of the Forest as theirs, owing to the bounds of the latter not often being viewed, but such gave them no legal rights. And what they did lay claim to was comparatively inconsiderable, so that the Forest as we know it today cannot be greatly altered in size from the Forest that was handed over to the officers of the Earl of Cornwall in 1240.

It will also be seen that in such parts of the moor where the Forest bounds have never been in dispute, such as on the Wallabrook, and the Dart, and the Wo Brook, the common land lying between them and the in-grounds is several miles in breadth. And it is certain that such was the case all round the Forest. To maintain that this was larger in 1240 than it now is, is to rob the border manors of their commons, which, in many instances, we know that they possessed long prior to that date.

The rights of the lord of the Forest over these commons are constantly shown in documents connected with it. Those of the manorial lords are fully recognised, but they run concurrently with the former. These ancient rights possessed by the holders of the great moor have never been relinquished, and the lord of Dartmoor is not only lord of the Forest, but also of its purlieus, 'the whiche wast and Comyns lyeth from the Forest vnto the Cornedyches, and hit ys callyd the Comyns of Devonshire.'

******

IV

THE LANDS OF ISABELLA DE FORTIBUS

On the 8th day of August, in the year 1276, an important deed, which affected a large tract of the border waste of western Dartmoor, was signed by Edward I. It was the confirmation of a gift of certain manors to Amicia, Countess of Devon, from her daughter Isabella, wife of William de Fortibus, Earl of Albemarle, and which comprehended within their bounds the extensive commons lying between the River Walkham and the Plym. These manors were relinquished by Isabella and conveyed by her to the countess to form part of the endowment by the latter of the abbey she was about to found, and which was to be called St. Benedict's of Buckland. They comprised Buckland, Bickleigh, and Walkhampton, with the advowson of the churches, and the Hundred of Roborough, with the service of free tenants, villeins, and others belonging to it, and all the appurtenances, liberties, and free customs. Included in the gift was the manor of Cullompton, in the east part of the county. The foundation deed was signed by the Lady Amicia in 1280, the abbey by that time having been built, and occupied by Cistercian monks brought by the countess from Quarr Abbey, in the Isle of Wight. After the death of Amicia her benefaction to the abbey was confirmed by her daughter in 1291. In her charter of confirmation Isabella, who had bestowed further property upon the abbey, mentions as then belonging to it the chapelry of Sheepstor and land in Sampford Spiney. The rich possessions have long since been alienated from the purposes of the donors, and the monks have departed from the groves of Buckland, but the name of Isabella de Fortibus is still associated with Dartmoor. Tradition, but in this case certainly with no degree of truth, has said that it was her hand that planted the oaks of Wistman, in the narrow valley of the West Dart. She died in 1292, the last of the ancient line of De Redvers.

The boundary of these lands, as traced in the charter, commences at Lobbapilla, or, as we now call it, Lopwell, on the Tavy, and runs up that river to its confluence with the Walkham, and thence to a point on that stream beyond Great Mis Tor. As it is only the moorland portion of the lands of the countess, and which formed the commons of Walkhampton and Sheepstor, with which we are concerned, we need not follow the boundary from Lopwell. We shall pass at once to the moor, making our way thither by the valley of the Walkham, through scenery of the most romantic description. From

Walkhampton village we take the road leading to Huckworthy Bridge, following it till we reach a lane branching to the right, and which will conduct us above the eastern bank of the stream to Long Ash Farm, on the verge of the commons.

At every step of the way there is that which will delight the eye. The sides of the deep and narrow valley are clothed with trees, and so thickly as to hide the stream from view; and above the trees rise the tors. Two clapper bridges are passed, spanning affluents of the Walkham, one of them being an exceedingly good example. This, which is figured in Moore's *History of Devon*, published in parts between 1829 and 1836, is crossed just before reaching Long Ash Farm, and consists of two openings, the pier and buttresses being very rude and massive. But it is before arriving at this bridge that the pedestrian encounters that which will afford him the greatest delight. It is where the road, rough in the extreme, passes Hucken Tor that the finest prospect of the many afforded by this upland walk is presented. As an example of Dartmoor border scenery it is not excelled in any part of the moorland region, and the rambler who chooses to set out from Yelverton or Horrabridge, and make his way by this path to the moor, will reap a rich reward. The fine mass of Vixen Tor across the valley, the bold outline of Great Mis Tor, the wilderness of grey boulders at the foot of King Tor, and the numerous other rock piles rearing their strange shapes against the sky, with a distant view, beyond the gorge, of field and farmstead, combine to form a picture that cannot fail to fill the beholder with the most pleasurable emotions, and to which the ivy draped rocks of Hucken Tor, rising midst the mountain ash, form a fitting centre.

From Long Ash Farm we descend to Merivale Bridge, and the open common being now before us, no impediments will present themselves to our making a companion of the stream which has hitherto been only our guide. And a cheerful companion it is as it glides rapidly onward, breaking into foam when it encounters the moss-covered rocks or runs merrily over the pebbles. But it is not always in a tranquil mood, and when the rains have swollen the tiny brooks which feed it, and they have increased its volume, it descends with a roar and has been known to claim its victims. Mr. A. B. Collier, of Carthamartha, informs us that on one occasion when on a fishing excursion on the moor the body of an elderly man, which had been found dead in the river, was brought into the wayside inn at Merivale Bridge while he was there. An inquest was held, and on the foreman of the jury being asked for the verdict, he announced as their finding, 'Died by the visitation of the Almighty, brought on by crossing the river when it was vlidded.'

Passing up the stream, with the rocks of Great Mis Tor towering high on the right, we find that it bends round the hill on which they are placed. Here we soon reach the Forest boundary, which crosses the Walkham less than a mile to the north of the tor at a spot to which a story attaches. A man who did not possess very great powers of discriminating between meum and teum was passing this way with a fine sheep to which he had helped himself from one of the flocks on the moor. He was carrying the animal on his shoulder, having secured its legs with a rope, but on clambering over a great rock which lay in his path its struggles caused him to stumble. In falling, the rope became twisted round his neck, and the weight of the sheep, which fell on the other side of the rock, so tightened it that the hangman's office was anticipated, and justice had obtained all she could have hoped to do in a court with the most clever of prosecuting counsel. From this circumstance the stone became known as Hanging Rock, and though the spot on the Walkham is not named in any of the Forest perambulations, it is yet sometimes so called. Unfortunately, for the story, it is related of so many rocks in England as to leave room for no other conclusion than that it is a pure invention, and that the meaning of the name should rather be looked for in the position of the rock, those which bear it usually being poised in a curious manner, either by natural or artificial means.

From this, the most northern point of the lands of the Countess Isabella, the boundary turns southward and runs conterminous with that of the Forest as far as the Plym, but is drawn in a direction the reverse of that followed by the perambulators of 1240. The intermediate bond-marks named in the charter, are Mistorpanna, the rock on Mis Tor in which is the great basin; and which thus seems to have been the particular pile that marked the boundary line; Hystochres, the Ysfother of the perambulation of 1240, and the Hisworthy of today; Crucem Siwardi, the cross of Siward, one of the finest of the early Christian memorials existing in the Forest; Gyllesburgh, called in 1240 Elysburghe, and now known as Eylesbarrow; and Plymcrundla, named in a document of later date, Plym Crundle. The record of this part of the boundary of the countess's lands, which agrees with the line of the Forest as returned in Henry III's time, is valuable as showing what considerable tracts of common land were attached to the border-manors.

When the good brothers of St. Benedict's, of Buckland, visited the furthermost bounds of their possessions and climbed to the great rock they called Mis Tor Pan, they would view not only much of their own domain, but also the broad lands of the neighbouring Abbey of Tavistock, founded some 300 years before their own. Even in those early times that town was of some importance, and this it has never lost, though it is said that such have been its vicissitudes that at one time so microscopical became the vicar's income that he was constrained to petition the parishioners for a pair of shoes. Tavistock not only took a prominent position as the seat of a religious house, and of a famous Saxon school, but also the proud one of possessing the first printing-press set up in Devon.

But it is to be feared that the spread of learning was not maintained, if the suggestion in a notice exhibited in the town some years ago by a certain tradesman was warranted. It was at the time that photography was in its infancy, and the principal studio there was nothing more than one of a few small wooden erections that stood in the open space in front of the present Townhall. One morning it was not opened as usual, but a notice affixed to the shutters explained the reason. It read thus: 'Gone to Launceston for a few days; those who can't read inquire next door.' It is satisfactory, at all events, to know that the photographer was able to write, and we presume he was scarcely like the border farmer's son whom we once knew. On our expressing surprise that he had not made greater progress in learning to read, we were quickly assured by his mother that he was by no means so backward as we supposed. 'Sampson hasn't got on very well with his speling,' she said, 'but he can write better than he can read.'

The monks may have derived considerable gratification in viewing their possessions from Mis Tor, that is if they ever took the trouble to climb up to it, but they could never have experienced any more real delight than that felt by the lover of nature who visits the huge cluster of rocks today. The views from all the Dartmoor border heights are extensive and varied, but they cannot all be looked upon from so romantic a standpoint as is afforded by the hoary piles of Mis Tor. From each frontier hill there is to be seen that wide expanse of cultivated country on the one hand, and the great dusky sweeps of moorland on the other, yet not one of these extensive prospects is wanting in some distinctive feature. From Mis Tor the meeting of the Tamar and the Tavy can be seen, and that great iron highway which Brunel threw across the united streams. Against the western sky rise the Cornish hills; eastward is a silent land, for there one looks into the heart of the grim old moor.

The next bound named in the charter is Hisworthy, the view from which we have already noticed, and we therefore pass on to the succeeding one. This is Siward's Cross, and we shall find it near the head of the valley in which the Swincombe River rises, its source being the well-known Fox Tor Mire. As this fine example of a Dartmoor cross is mentioned by the perambulators of 1240 as a Forest bond-mark, we know for a certainty that it was standing at that date, and as the bounds were then the same as they had been in Henry I's time, we may not unreasonably conclude that it was in existence in that Monarch's reign. But it is probable that it belongs to an even earlier period, and that the name it bears, and which is inscribed in faint characters upon it, is that of a holder of lands near this part of the moor in Saxon times. This was none other than Siward the Dane, who was created Earl of Northumberland by the Confessor, and who numbered among his possessions the manors of Tavy and Warne, in Devonshire. As the Forest appears to have been under grant to a subject at the beginning of the 13th century, the charter of John being signed while he was Earl of Mortaigne, there is no apparent reason why, in earlier times, it may not also have been temporarily conferred upon those whom the King desired to reward. Upon the great Siward, son of Bearn, the hunting ground of which the waste of his own manors went to form a part, may well have been bestowed, and in the solitary cross at the head of the Swincombe Valley we may see a bond-mark of the great Earl who governed the northern province of the Confessor with such vigour and ability.

On the western face of the cross is another name, which in a note on the back of an old map of Dartmoor, now in the Albert Memorial Museum, at Exeter, is given as Roolande, but which has also been read as Bod Bond and as Booford. In 1883, when conducting some antiquarian investigations on Dartmoor, we examined the inscription with great care, and reading in the light of the medieval history of this part of the moor, came to the conclusion that the letters had not been correctly deciphered. That they were cut upon the cross by the good brothers of St. Bendedict's there is little doubt, and none that they represent the name of the place where the abbey stood, though in its older form. The word which has puzzled so many is Boclond, written in two lines across the shaft, and our opinion, expressed at the time, has been endorsed by all who have since noticed the cross. How such a mistake could have been made by those who described the cross on the back of the old map it is not easy to see, especially as the latter is considered to be of 15th century date, and was consequently drawn within 200 years of the monks of Buckland taking possession of their manors. It is probable that the illegibility of the map is really the cause of the error. In places it has been retouched, and some 'restorer,' who knew nothing of the locality, may have turned Boclond into Roolande.

Nun's, or Siward's, Cross

At the present time Siward's Cross is more generally referred to as Nun's Cross, a name which I have elsewhere ventured to suggest may be a corruption of the Cornu-Celtic word 'nans,' a valley or dale, and was thus possibly derived from its situation. This, however, is conjecture, for the name may not really be a very ancient one. We first meet with it – or a form of it – in 1699, when the cross is referred to by Quintin Brown, the yeoman of whom we have already made mention, as Nannecross.

In 1846 Siward's Cross was overturned and broken by two lads when searching for cattle on the moor, but was shortly afterwards repaired by a stonemason named John Newcombe. In September, 1889, one of those who helped to throw it down was seen by Mr. W. H. Woodley, of Plymouth. He was then working on the railway, near Bickleigh Station, and on being questioned on the matter shewed much concern, evidently fearful that even after the lapse of so long a time he was to be made to answer for his act. The cross is 7 feet 4 inches high, and is fixed in a socket-stone, the surface of which is level with the ground. It is easily reached from Princetown, there being a plainly-marked track leading to it; the distance is under 3 miles.

The next bound is marked by the tumuli on Eylesbarrow, where the parishes of Walkhampton and Sheepstor meet on the line of the Forest, and on passing this mark a descent is made to the Plym. In the charter of the countess the boundary is said to run from Gyllesburgh, or Eylesbarrow, to Plymcrundla, and thence to the Plym, an object thus being named as a bond-mark which does not find a mention in the record of any Forest perambulation. But we know that it must have been on the boundary of the Forest, because such was conterminous with the Countess Isabella's possessions, and if we can identify Plymcrundla it will enable us to fix almost with certainty the line which the perambulators of 1240 took when they passed from Grymsgrove to Eylesbarrow.

On the old map, the names on which are not like the charter in Latin, Plymcrundla appears as Plym Crundle, but what object is intended is not shown. The name itself is, however, sufficient to tell us this. Bannister, in his Cornish Glossary, gives 'Crundle-Crundwell, a spring, or well, with a basin,' and it is to the Cornu-Celtic, we must look for the meaning of most of the ancient place-names on Dartmoor. There is a tiny rivulet falling into the Plym a short distance above Evil Combe, and a straight line drawn from Grymsgrove to Eylesbarrow would fall almost along its course. The name of Plym Crundle would very well describe it, since it is one of the springs of that river, and that we see in it the bond-mark mentioned in the charter of Isabella de Fortibus there can scarcely be a doubt.

Down this rivulet we pass to the Plym, here only a small stream, yet soon to have its waters augmented by the brooks that pour their tribute from the hills. Tranquil now, its amber waters telling of the peat from which it has but lately oozed, it rolls lazily along, but ere it has gone far upon its course it will fume and fret among the boulders. Yet only for a time will its mood be turbulent. When it reaches the groves of Bickleigh the roar with which it swept by the Dewerstone will have subsided to a gentle murmur, as it glides evenly onward to expand into the estuary of the Laira, and greet the 'notable old town' to which it gives name.

For a distance of about 4 miles the Plym formed the line of demarcation between the lands with which Buckland Abbey was endowed and the commons lying within the bounds of the parish of Shaugh. A considerable portion of the latter had also belonged to the De Redvers family, the tract lying on the left bank of the Plym, and forming what is now known as Trowlesworthy Warren, having been granted by a representative of that house to Sampson de Traylesworthy, prior to the reign of Edward I. A small tributary stream, called in the charter the Yaddabrook, but not now known by that name, falls into the Plym less than a mile above Cadaford Bridge, and this became the boundary for a short distance. Then leaving it, the line was carried to the south and west of Ringmoor Down, and thence by Smallacombe to the Mew, which it touched not far above the present Marchants Bridge, near Meavy.

But before leaving the Plym it may be well to remark that the name by which it is sometimes called in that part of its course extending for a mile or two above Shaugh Bridge is wrongly applied to it. We find it spoken of as the Cad, though never so on the moor; but so far as we have been able to discover, the name was not in use before 1804. In that year Howard's poem of *Bickleigh Vale* appeared, and it is there we meet with it. But there is actually no such river as the Cad, though that name, having once been brought into use, still survives. How did the mistake arise? We read that of old the Ephraimites fell victims to their own bad pronunciation; the Plym lost its name through the bad pronunciation of others.

To explain this we must trace the river up to the bridge over which passes the road leading from Shaugh to Meavy. It is known as Cadover, or Cadaford, Bridge, the latter name gradually taking the place of the former. By a process of reasoning somewhat similar to that which has been supposed to prove an eel pie to be a pigeon, Cadover Bridge was regarded as the bridge over the Cad, and so upon the Plym was bestowed a name which in its modern signification is not attractive. But this would probably not have occurred had not the name of this bridge been corrupted. Near to it is the farm of Cadworthy, and that the bridge anciently bore a similar name is abundantly clear from the charter of Isabella de Fortibus in which it appears as the 'ponte de Cadaworth.' The river is mentioned several times, and always by the name of the Plym, and parts of it are referred to from near its source to a considerable distance below Bickleigh Bridge. Its confluence with the Mew, below the Dewerstone, is spoken of as the place where Mewy falls in Plymma, so that the evidence is conclusive that such was its ancient name, and in later records of the moor it bears no other.

The boundary of the lands conveyed to the abbey by the countess ran from the foot of Smallacombe up the Mew to Olyaka, by which name, though it cannot be positively identified, the Sheepstor Brook, which falls into the Mew below Burrator, may possibly be meant. On passing south of Sheepstor village the boundary turned to the north-east, and was carried across the common to the Dean Combe Water, or Narrator Brook as it is often called, and thence once more to the Mew. Much of the parish of Sheepstor, including the village and the well-known tor of the same name, lay outside the boundary. It was the chapelry and not the manor that was given by the countess to the house at

Buckland.

It is said that the manor of Sheepstor was formerly under an obligation to keep a turret of Plympton Castle in repair, which may possibly have been the condition on which certain privileges were conferred on the inhabitants. In a note to Carrington's poem of *Dartmoor* these are set forth from a record dated 1626, in which they are described as the 'ancient privileges and freedom of the manor of Sheepstor,' and included among others the exemption of those who dwelt in the 'hamlet' from the duty of watching and warding all beacons, save those in the same 'hamlet.' Sheepstor continued to be a chapelry attached to Bickleigh until 1877. The dedication is unknown but the former existence of a well nearby, which bore the name of St. Leonard's Well, has led to the supposition that this was the patron saint.

Sheepstor village and tor.

In the days when there was no resident vicar in the parish it might well be imagined that the pulpit of Sheepstor Church was not occupied quite so frequently as at present. Indeed, according to the old story it was only once a month that a service was held there. We know not how this may be, but if the same story be not a story it was not always suffered to remain empty merely because the visits of the minister happened to be so few and far between. One Sunday morning, to the great surprise of the clerk, the parson was seen entering the churchyard. 'Way, you bant com' to hold sarvice, sir, be 'ee?' asked the clerk. 'Not come to conduct service? Of course that is what I am here for,' answered the parson. 'But it bant your day, sir. You'm avaur your time; I didn't think to zee 'ee till next Zinday.' 'Bless me! Have I made a mistake? Well, never mind; since I am here we will certainly hold the service.' 'But you can't praich, sir,' said the clerk. 'Can't preach! Why what do you mean?'

Pixies' Cave, Sheeps Tor

asked the bewildered parson. 'Well, sir, you can't now, I tell 'ee,' replied the clerk. 'Tis like this heer. My ole guze be a settin' a brude in the pulpit, an' her wasn't hatch mun till next Wednesday, zo you can't do no praichin' to-day.'

At the southern foot of the great tor which rises behind the village is the celebrated Pixies' Cave, the entrance to which is concealed by the clatter of rocks which here covers the whole slope. It is stated in a note in Polwhele's *Devon*, published at the end of the 18th century, that during the Civil Wars this cave formed the hiding-place of one of the Elfords, who were seated at Longstone, in this parish. The tradition of the fugitive Royalist concealing himself in the hollow trunk of a tree, or cave, and being secretly supplied with food, is met with in more than one locality, and it may therefore not be wise to place too much credence in the Sheepstor story. Elford was said to have made his imprisonment in the grotto a little more tolerable by passing his time in painting on its granite walls, and Mr. Yonge, of Puslinch, informed Polwhele that he had been told by an elderly gentleman that the paintings were very fresh in his time. This was probably in the gentleman's youth, for when Mr. E. A. Bray visited the cave in 1802 he saw no traces of them.

A low, narrow passage a few feet in length gives admittance to the home of the pixies. In this passage is a turning leading directly into a small, square chamber, in which a man might remain comfortably concealed, though its height is scarcely sufficient to permit him to stand upright. The walls are regular and comparatively smooth, and on one side is a naturally-formed stone bench or seat. If Elford did here find security from the followers of Cromwell, he would at will be able to cast off that 'cribbed, cabined, and confined' feeling to which his rocky abode would naturally give rise. He had only to step to the entrance of his cavern, when his eyes would rest upon as fair a view as any in broad Devon. On one side the tors above the valley of the Plym, and the wide commons, and beyond the commons, fields and woods, and still further away the blue waters of the Channel. At the foot of the hills rising against the western sky, was the Lynher, like a lake embosomed in trees, and stretching northward the moorlands of Eastern Cornwall. Across the valley of the Mew was Yennadon, with its steep, heathery slope and grey crags, and almost at his feet the tiny village and ancient church to which men had given the name borne by the tor in the bosom of which he had found an asylum.

Years have passed away since any of the Elford family were seen in Sheepstor, and the peasantry will also tell you that it was 'a mortal long while agone' that the pixies visited it. But if those merry little elves have ceased to gambol on the sward at midnight, and to fly through the keyholes and tease the lazy serving-maids, something of the supernatural is left in the country of stream and tor. Strange sounds heard in lonely places at night are ascribed to 'the sperits,' and it is well to know that by such simple means as drawing a line on the ground, or crossing a brook or stream, repeating at the same time the Lord's Prayer, they may be kept from troubling. One old moorman appears to have been a firm believer in the efficacy of prayer when in danger of molestation by ghostly visitants, though it is to be feared he seldom practised what he pinned his faith to. Hearing one dark night on the moor some unearthly sounds near him, and being at a loss to understand their cause, he was terror-stricken, and imagined the spirits were pursuing him. 'I could'n rin no more'n a cheel,' he said; 'Zo I vlinged myzel among the vuz, out o' sight, an' tried to zay 'Our Vayther,' but I could'n mine un.'

From the Mew the boundary line ran to Yanedone, or, as we now call it, Yennadon, Cross, which, there is good reason to believe, stood not very far from the head of the lane leading from Dousland to Walkhampton. There it was carried to Lake, and on by Gratton to Elford Lake, and once more to the Mew. But it is not our purpose to trace it through the cultivated country, our notice extending only to that portion of the gift which comprised the commons of Walkhampton and Sheepstor. It is sufficient to state that the Mew formed the boundary for a considerable distance, and that the line ran up the hill to the south of Shaugh, to Hawk Tor on Shaugh Common, and turning, crossed the river lower down and went to Woolwell, a farm about 4 miles from Plymouth. Then the forerunner of the present Tavistock road became the boundary to a point beyond the village of Roborough, whence the line was continued by way of Bickham to Lopwell, thus completing the circuit. It will be seen that the gift included, besides the two commons named above, the whole of Roborough Down. The more valuable lands were, of course, those in the parishes of Buckland and Bickleigh, where the climate and the soil afforded scope for the efforts of the husbandman, and also in the valley below Walkhampton village, where similar conditions prevailed. The wastes, though having their uses as hunting-grounds of the abbots, and as affording pasturage for the cattle of the free tenants, brought little revenue to the abbey.

The boundary of the Dartmoor possessions of the countess from the point to which we have traced it on the Mew, ran over the southern shoulder of Peak Hill, and thence in a northerly direction to the Walkham. The road from Dousland to Princetown passes through the centre of these common lands, and though their full extent cannot be seen, a good idea of it may be gained. The hills hide much from view, but with the exception of the giant Sheepstor and the downs across the valley of the Walkham, nothing is seen until Princetown is reached but what lay within the boundary set forth in the charter. With the signing of the deed of gift by the Lady Amicia, and the confirmation by her daughter, Isabella de Fortibus, these extensive commons bordering for so great a distance the western limits of the Forest of Dartmoor, passed from the great house of De Redvers to the Abbey of St. Benedict's of Buckland.

Although neighbours of the Benedictines of Tavistock, in the sense that their possessions adjoined, the monks of Buckland do not appear to have always been on the best of terms with them, if we may judge from a circumstance recorded by Miss Rachel Evans in her *Home Scenes*. That writer does not give the date of the occurrence, but says she gathered the particulars of it from an old document. From these we learn that the Abbot of Tavistock was the owner of Blackmoreham Wood, close to the beautiful confluence of the Tavy and the Walkham, and that a weir thrown across the river there belonged to Robert, Abbot of Buckland. One day the forester, in whose charge the Wood of Blackmoreham was placed, was surprised to find there, at a spot called Ivy Oak, the Abbot of Buckland with a number of his monks felling the trees. The forester, whose name it seems was Thomas de Gryreband, like a faithful servant, sought to protect his lord's property; but possibly, as it is stated that his anger rose, he may have commanded the monks to desist in terms more forcible than polite. At all events the ire of the monks was also aroused, for after 'insulting' him, they added injury. They beat him, and wounded him in the right arm with an arrow, then, not content with that, they robbed him of his coat. Gryreband, shewing some of the prudence he might possibly have exercised earlier with advantage, made his escape, and informed his master of the circumstance. Satisfaction must be obtained, and so the Abbot of Tavistock instituted a suit against his neighbour of Buckland. The defendants, among whom were William de Norwy, John de la Burgh, and Brother Nicholas, said that the Abbot of Buckland had a right to cut a sufficient number of branches in Blackmoreham Wood to repair his weir, and that while doing so the forester insulted and attacked them. It was true they had carried away his coat, but they repudiated the charge of theft. Gryreband had run away, they pleaded, and thus left his garment 'in their charge.' They were each fined one mark and 'acquitted.' Thomas the forester was fined a mark and a half, a decision which, if not very convincing as to its justice, would at least prove, though probably to his dissatisfaction, the uncertainty of the law.

But it was not only with the Benedictines of Tavistock that the abbots of Buckland had disputes. In 1318 we find there was some disagreement between one of them and Hugh de Audley, at that time a grantee of the Forest. The Abbot, who was apparently a lover of the chase, had taken upon himself to hunt within the confines of the latter, and in consequence a commission was issued to inquire into the circumstances and effect a settlement. About this period other matters besides those concerning the right to hunt were in dispute, and possibly the question of boundaries was one. But the encroachments, if such there were, were not on the part of the commoners, or we should not find them petitioning for a perambulation of the Forest to be made. They would scarcely have shewn a desire that the boundary should be viewed, had they been in fault. Whether this perambulation ever took place does not appear, but if so, and the return to it could be found, its comparisons with that of 1240 would be most interesting.

In the reign of Edward III an abbot of Buckland was again involved in a dispute concerning his commons. It appears that the foresters had entered upon them and found estrays there, for which the abbot had been indicted at Lydford. The latter consequently complained to Edward, the Black Prince, who was then lord of Dartmoor, that his commons had been invaded, and the Prince issued a commission to inquire into the alleged trespass. It is probable that the result was not favourable to the abbot, for the foresters seem only to have been exercising the right which belonged to their lord of driving the purlieus of the Forest.

One hundred and twenty years later, namely in 1478, there was another dispute in which the Abbot of Buckland figured. This was Thomas Oliver, who is said to have interfered with the right of the commoners to depasture on the moor. It is stated that he claimed over 10,000 acres 'of the King's land in the Forest and waste of Dartmoor.' This cannot, of course, mean that the abbot endeavoured to possess himself of a fresh tract of land of that extent, but that he claimed the sole right to the commons within the bounds of his manors, and which were of that acreage. Over these the men of Devon had possessed rights of pasturage long before they were given to the De Redvers. They had always been recognised, and the grant to the abbey could not effect them. The jury, by whom the case was determined, found for the King and the commoners, and 'agaynest the foresaid Abbot of Monkenbuclond.' The case is one of considerable importance as shewing that the lord of the Forest had also rights over its purlieus.

The jury who made the survey in 1609 refer to the great stretch of common land which we have here been noticing, as we shall see when we come to trace its later history. Then we shall find it in the hands of others than monks, notwithstanding that the Lady Amicia gave her manors to them to hold 'well and peaceably for ever.' But at present we leave these western purlieus in the safe keeping of the good brothers of St. Benedict's of Buckland, while we turn our attention to another part of the moor.

*****

V

LYDFORD LAW

On the death of Richard Plantagenet he was succeeded in the Earldom of Cornwall by his eldest son, Henry, who, however, only held it until 1271, in which year he was assassinated while on his return from the Holy Land. His brother Edmund became his successor, and also holder of the manor of Lydford and the Forest of Dartmoor, which he is named on the Hundred Rolls as possessing. It does not appear from Domesday whether there was a manor of Lydford at the time that survey was made, as only the borough is there mentioned. But we hear of one, or, at all events, of a reputed manor, in 1227, when we find it named in a writ of Henry III commanding William Briwere, the custodian of Lydford Castle and of Dartmoor, to permit the market at Lydford, which had been discontinued, to be again held there. The manor and castle were also named in the grant of the Forest by the King to the Earl of Cornwall in 1239, the words of the charter being 'all that our manor of Lydford, with the castle of the same place, and all its appurtenances, together with the Forest of Dartmoor, and all the appurtenances of the same Forest.'

Although the Forest Courts could no longer be held when Dartmoor was severed from the Crown, there was a kind of survival of them in the courts held by the Earls of Cornwall. These had jurisdiction over the manor and Forest, which have been associated since they first came into the hands of a subject, and to some extent over the border commons as well. Presentments were made at these Lydford Courts for acts of trespass, such as the taking away of peat by those who did not possess the right to do so, for destroying the pasture by burning, for stopping up paths, and neglecting to repair gates and for leaving them open; for the wrongful agistment of cattle, and for driving away the cattle of others and impounding them; for enclosing land without authority; for not assisting at the drifts and other matters, the most important of which was the hunting and killing the deer. Those in whose charge the Forest was placed were probably very strict in enforcing the law, and though the old forestal jurisdiction was ended, the powers of the Earls of Cornwall was not suffered to be forgotten. The important privileges they possessed are due, it has been supposed, to their having succeeded to the rights of the old British princes.

Earl Edmund died in 1300, and leaving no issue, the Forest reverted to the

Crown, and remained in its possession until the reign of Edward III, though during this period it was sometimes in the hands of grantees, of whom Piers de Gaveston was one. The year 1336 was marked by an event of some importance in the history of Dartmoor, for on the 17th March Edward III raised the Earldom of Cornwall into a Duchy, and the status of its lords underwent a change. The first duke was his son Edward, afterwards the Black Prince, and in the charter creating the Duchy the reversion of the castle and manor of Lydford, with the chase of Dartmoor, was granted to him. The Earls of Cornwall had held these of the King at fee farm, paying therefor £10 yearly, but henceforth they were to be held in chief and knight service, as parcel of the Duchy of Cornwall.

Prince Edward did not come into possession of Lydford and Dartmoor until 6 years after the date of the charter. At the time it was granted they were in the hands of Hugh de Audley, Earl of Gloucester, and Margaret his wife, who was the niece of Edward II, and they had been given to them by that Monarch for the term of Margaret de Audley's life. She died in 1342, and by a writ dated 21st July of that year the Sheriff of Devon was commanded by the King to give possession of the castle, manor, and chase of Dartmoor to Prince Edward. According to an Inquisition taken about that time they were worth yearly £45. 12s. 6d.

The law as administered at Lydford had early an evil reputation, which even in the days when that place owned the Black Prince for its lord had become proverbial. In some lines which Thomas Wright in his *Political Poems* considers to have been written in 1399, a reference to the law of Lydford occurs, and it is certain that the harshness which prevailed in its courts, where justice existed only in name, originated in times long before those of the hero of Poictiers. In later days William Browne, one of Devon's sons of song, wrote a humorous poem describing a visit to Lydford made by him about the year 1644. He tells us that he had often heard of Lydford Law, and though in his time it was much less severe than formerly, we learn quite sufficient from his account to convince us that it had by no means entirely lost its original character.

In Ray's Collection of Proverbs we have the saying relative to the justice meted out at the Castle of Dartmoor, as the ancient stronghold is sometimes called in the Forest records.

"First hang and draw,
Then hear the cause, is Lydford Law."

That such a course of procedure ever existed few would be inclined to believe. Most would probably be disposed to regard the saying only as being intended to convey the idea that the law administered at Lydford Castle was rigorous and unjust, and not as one to be accepted literally. But there is much more truth in the proverb than might at first be imagined. There is, in fact, little doubt that punishment actually was inflicted upon offenders before sentence had been passed upon them by the court.

To understand this we must go back to the Norman period, for the law which obtained at Lydford and gave to it its unenviable name was that which had its origin in the forestal system. Lydford was a place of importance before the arrival of the Conqueror, and in all probability was a seat of judicature in Saxon times, but there is no reason for supposing that its laws, framed though they might have been to protect the deer on the uplands of Dartmoor, were tyrannically unjust. They were not as those made by the man who, the old chronicler tells us, loved the red deer so greatly that he had been called their father. It is unlikely that Lydford, where the burgesses fought stoutly for their town after the Siege of Exeter, became the home of despotism before the imposition of the cruel Forest Laws by the Norman Kings.

The worst offence a man could commit in a Forest was that of killing the deer, or other of the animals which were hunted. As, however, all other offences were considered to be indirectly to the hurt of the deer, they were regarded as being scarcely less heinous. The Forest Courts, which dealt with all cases of Forest breach, consisted of the Court of Attachments, the Court of Swainmote and the Court of Justice Seat. The first was held every 40 days, when presentments were made by the foresters to the verderers who composed it. The latter were officers appointed by writ of the King, and there were four to each Forest. At the Court of Swainmote the verderers formed the bench, and the jury, which was empanelled from the Forest freeholders, or, as they are called on Dartmoor, the Forest tenants, considered the presentments from the foresters, and those also from the Attachment Courts, the duty of the latter being only to prepare cases. The steward of the Court of Swainmote, who was skilled in the law, sat as assessor. If the jury did not consider the evidence sufficiently strong to warrant them in sending the case before the higher Court of Justice Seat, it was discharged. If, on the contrary, they found the presentment true, it was sent before that tribunal in order that sentence might be passed.

The Court of Swainmote was held three times yearly, and the Court of Justice Seat once in 3 years. Over the latter one of the Chief Justices of Forests presided, assisted by a common law judge. Prisoners found guilty by the Dartmoor Court of Swainmote were detained in Lydford Castle, and if it so happened that the Court of Justice Seat had been held not long previously to their trial, they would, of course, have to wait nearly 3 years before it again assembled, and were thus punished by imprisonment before sentence was passed.

But all Forest Law was the same throughout the country, and harsh as the proceedings may seem, there would appear to be no reason why the Lydford Courts should have gained a worse reputation than others. The reason is probably to be found in the corruption of those who became the gaolers of the unfortunate prisoners awaiting trial. Such of them as were able to furnish a sufficient bribe were permitted to go at large, for the Sheriff had power to bail prisoners, while those whose means would not permit them to satisfy the cupidity of their captors, were in some cases kept in bondage, and in others, it is to be feared, were made to suffer the penalties which it was known awaited them when the next court should assemble. The keepers of Lydford Castle, in short, anticipated the sentence of the Court of Justice Seat, and when that tribunal met, and the cases were brought before them, they would pass judgement on men who had suffered the penalty long before, and thus the proverb was substantially true.

That those in whose hands authority was placed were often guided by anything but a sense of justice there is abundant evidence to show. The charter of 1204, as already remarked, clearly proves that abuses in the administration of the law existed, and that the men of Devon had complained of them to King John. After purporting to disafforest the county outside the bounds of Dartmoor, the King refers to certain duties of the Sheriff, and directs how he is to proceed. He was to make one 'turn' each year, to inquire concerning pleas of the Crown, 'without hindrance made to anyone.' Except for the attachment of pleas of the Crown when they should happen with the coroners, or for assuring the peace, no more 'turns' were to be made. 'So, indeed,' the words of the charter run, 'that in that Eyre he should take nothing to his own use.' All prisoners whom the county might be willing to take upon itself to bail were to be set at large, 'so that they be not any longer detained in prison through the malice or hindrance of the Sheriff.' The charter further set forth that if the Sheriff should be convicted of acting unjustly towards the men of Devon he should be fined and removed from his position.

From this it is easy to gather that the Sheriffs had been in the habit of exceeding their duties, and using their power to their own advantage, without regard to the rights of those who were unfortunate enough to find themselves in their custody. If effect had been given to the charter, the remedy desired by the men of Devon would have been provided; but unfortunately John thought more of the payment he was to receive from them for granting it than he did of redressing their wrongs. The laws which regulated all matters pertaining to Dartmoor continued to be oppressive and cruel, for when the forestal system began to wane, and the prisoners no longer suffered the loss of their eyes, or were put to death, for killing the deer, rigorous treatment continued to be meted out to captives who had offended against other laws. These were the enactments concerning the Stannaries, or tin mining district, of Devon, which will hereafter demand out notice. While the tinners' laws were in operation there was little chance of Lydford losing the name it had earned by its administration of those regulating the affairs of the Royal Forest.

In a charter to the tinners of the 33rd of Edward I Lydford is named as the Stannary prison, and also in a Parliament Roll of the 50th of Edward III. In the latter the 'poor commonalty of the county of Devon' petition the King to remedy certain evils which they suffer at the hands of the tinners. Among other matters, they desire to be informed what is intended by the following clause of the first-named charter, which relates to tinners who have transgressed, and their imprisonment by the Warden of the Stannaries: 'And if any of the tinners aforesaid shall be delinquent in any matter for which they ought to be imprisoned, they shall be arrested by the Warden aforesaid and detained in our prison at Lydford, and not elsewhere, until they shall be delivered, according to the law and custom of our realm.'

The petitioners go on to say that tinners who have been arrested for felony, and placed in the custody of the warden are often suffered to go at large. They also state that there was then (1377) no gaol delivery at Lydford oftener than once in 10 years, so that it is evident that an even worse state of things existed, with regard to imprisonment before trial, than in the days of the old Forest Courts. But what the petitioners characterise as being worse than all is the construction which the warden places on the words 'not elsewhere,' for they say he takes those tinners who have been imprisoned for debt out of other prisons, and sends them to Lydford, and that they are then never compelled to make satisfaction to those to whom they are indebted.

Here we have Lydford Law in another aspect. In place of being excessively severe it is criminally indulgent. But this favouritism was not extended to any other than tinners, and, probably, not to them if they had been guilty of anything calculated to injure the mining interests. This is shown in the treatment accorded to Richard Strode, member of Parliament for Plympton, in the reign of Henry VIII, who, being made prisoner by the tinners, was cast into an underground dungeon in Lydford Castle, and had he not bribed his gaoler would have been kept on bread and water and heavily ironed. As it was, his treatment was quite sufficient to prove that Lydford Law did not err on the side of leniency when the supposed rights of the tinners were attacked. The tyrannical Sir Richard Grenville was governor of the castle for the King during the Civil wars, and it is also said that the infamous Jeffreys presided in its courts, so that its evil character seems to have been constantly maintained.

Lydford was one of the four towns in Devon that possessed a mint in Saxon times, and was then otherwise a place of note. It is said to have suffered severely at the hands of the Danes, who made their way there after having burnt Tavistock Abbey, in 997. This would, however, appear to have only temporarily affected its fortunes, for in the following century we find it to be equal in importance to the large towns of the county, as the entry in Domesday respecting it will show. 'The King has a Borough, Lideford. King Edward held it in demesne. There are 28 burgesses within the borough, and 41 outside. Among them all they render to the King 60s. by weight, and they have two carucates of land outside the borough. There are 40 houses waste since the King came into England. If an expedition goes by land or by sea it renders as much service as Barnstaple and Totness.' The town was anciently enclosed by a wall, the foundations of which, according to Risdon, were to be seen in the beginning of the 17th century. It formerly sent members to Parliament, though not after the reign of Edward III, for its glories are all of a far-away time. One vestige, however, of its early importance remained to it down to about 150 years ago. This was its Mayor and Corporation, and when these had departed

Lydford bade farewell to all its greatness.

Lydford Castle, the notorious Stannary Prison

Lydford Castle, the square keep of which alone remains, stands on a mound, at one end of the village, and above the deep gorge of the Lyd. In a ruinous condition today, it is somewhat remarkable that in many of the references to it, it is described as being in a similar state. In an inquisition taken after the death of Edmund, Earl of Cornwall, in 1300, it is mentioned as 'a certain ruinous castle, the easements of which do not suffice to its sustenation'; and in an account of the borough, in 1344, the castle is stated to have been in ruins, but that it had then undergone repair. In Queen Elizabeth's reign there are also references to its dilapidated condition. A survey, which included the borough, taken in 1618, describes it as 'an ancient castle, in which the prison for the Stannary of Devon and Forest of Dartmoor hath been always kept, until of late that it was removed by reason that the castle grew ruinous.' William Browne says, in his fanciful way, that he took it for an old windmill. During the Commonwealth there was a Parliamentary survey of the borough of Lydford, made on the 27th August, 1650, in which the castle was said to be very much in decay and almost totally ruined. The floors were in a bad state of repair, and the principal beams had fallen; the roof was, however, not in a ruinous condition, as it had been recently covered with lead. In 1703 a report was made to the Treasury respecting the castle, which, in the opinion of the surveyor, had not been repaired since 1650. Nothing then remained but the bare walls, the lead and timber of the roof 'having been pillaged by the poor people, who abounded in the neighbouring country, being adjacent to Dartmoor'.

Subsequently the castle was again put in a state of repair, a court of survey to inquire into the customs and boundaries of the manor and Forest being held there in 1786, and other Duchy courts until a later date. Now it has once more become a ruin, and though presenting nothing particularly attractive in itself, cannot fail to awake an interest in those who have made themselves acquainted with its history. The sunlight now penetrates where once was gloom, and happy birds warble where only the groans of captives were heard of yore. Bolts and bars have long since rusted away, and the prison doors have dropped from their hinges and decayed; the pure breeze from the hills plays around the naked walls; and it is no longer true that Lydford Castle is, as once it was described, 'one of the moste annoyous, contagious, and detestable places within the realme.'

*****

VI

THE STANNARY OF DEVON

Of those who have made Dartmoor the scene of their labours none have been more busy than the tin-seeker. The efforts of the hill farmer have been restricted to a comparatively limited area on the moor, for he was bound by considerations of climate and soil, but the miner has been everywhere. There is not a valley, nor even a combe through which a rivulet trickles, in which he has not left traces of his presence. That he sought these silent uplands for the coveted ore at a remote period there are good grounds for believing, though but little light is let in upon the history of those far-off days. But there came a time when his operations were to be recorded, and the writings have come down to our own, and enable us to learn something of his work upon the moor during several centuries.

The earliest references to the mining on Dartmoor are found in a record in the Pipe Roll of the 8th of Richard I, 1197, and in a charter of the following year. It is true that in neither of these is there any mention of the moor, but they relate to the production of tin in Devon and Cornwall, and it is certain that the part of Devon in which that metal was found was Dartmoor. The charter is particularly interesting as showing that even in that day the tinners possessed ancient rights and that the profits of the mines had then long been an appanage of the Crown. From the Pipe Roll we learn that the mining was farmed out, and that the Stannary, or mining district, of Devon, was of greater value than the Stannary of Cornwall. We have it in an account for the year above-named, rendered by Philip de Haukeehirche and Harveius de Helion, which shews that the rental of the former was £100, and that of the latter £66. 13s. 4d. Tithe on this amount was granted by King John to the Bishops of Exeter, but the sum paid to them – £16. 14s. 4d. – afterwards became a fixed one.

In the charter the Sheriff of Devon is commanded by Hubert, Archbishop of Canterbury, on behalf of King Richard, to commit the Stannaries to the custody of William de Wrotham, and to cause him 'to hold the Tinners in that freedom which they ought, and have been accustomed to have.' Among other matters it provides for the weighing and stamping of the tin. Each 8 pounds of refined tin were to be regarded as the produce of 9 pounds of that metal as brought from the blowing-houses, or places where it had been smelted, and this was said to be according to 'the just and ancient weight of the City of

Exeter.' The refining, which was termed the 'second smelting,' and the weighing and stamping, were to take place at a building set aside for the purpose in certain of the towns of the county, and this could not be done elsewhere by anyone, as he valued his person and his goods. There were two appointed weighers, and also a clerk, who acted on behalf of the King. The stamp was to be kept under the seal of the Keeper of the Weights, and he and the clerk were to carefully record all the weighings that were made. When these regulations had been complied with and the dues had been paid, including one mark for every thousand-weight, which the King received 'as well as the ancient custom of the farm of tin,' the owner might remove his metal, unless the King exercised his right of pre-emption. The treasurers to whom the dues were paid, and who received them in the presence of the Keeper of the Weights and the clerk, made entries not only of the money, but of the quantity of tin weighed, as a check upon the keeper and the clerk, and also recorded the names of all traders who bought tin. The moneys received by them were paid over to the Chief Warden of the Stannaries.

To guard against the evasion of payment of the dues there were several stringent regulations. No 'man or woman, Christian or Jew,' was permitted to buy or sell any tin as it came from the blowing-house, or to remove it from the Stannary, unless it had first been weighted and stamped, nor to have it in their possession without this being done longer than a fortnight. Nor after being stamped could they keep this unrefined tin beyond 13 weeks. It had then to be taken to the appointed place, and the dues paid to the treasurers. In the ports of Devon and Cornwall persons were appointed to take the oaths of mariners, who might arrive there, that they would not receive on board their vessels any tin unless it had been duly weighed and stamped, and for the removal of which out of the two counties the owner possessed the licence of the Chief Warden of the Stannaries.

In 1201 King John granted a charter to the tinners in confirmation of their already existing privileges, which have been described as depending in some respects upon Royal charters, also upon common right and upon usages and customs. In his reign the Stannary of Devon increased in value, for in 1213 the rental of the farm of tin was £200. Among the privileges possessed by the tinners was that of taking peat from Dartmoor, for the purpose of smelting the ore. In a writ 3rd of Henry III, 1219, William Briwere is commanded 'to permit the men of Joan, Queen of England, to dig, burn, and lead away from the turbary of Dartmoor to her Stannaries, as they used and ought'; and in 1222 the King ordered that no one should hinder the tinners of Devon from taking fuel on the moor for their Stannary, as they had been accustomed to do. The peat is said to have been prepared in a certain manner, so as to produce carbonisation, and it frequently appears in the accounts of the rentals as 'coal.' It was admirably adapted for smiths, rendering the iron more durable than that which had been subjected to the heat of an ordinary coal fire.

The tin ore was obtained by a process known as streaming. The gravel con-

The remains of a blowing-house

taining it was placed on an inclined plane down which a stream of water was allowed to run, and which carried away the grit, leaving the particles of ore behind. The blowing-houses were erected near the stream-works, and the ruins of many are found on Dartmoor today. They are usually small, oblong buildings, with the doorway in one corner, and, in many cases, the moulds into which the smelted tin was poured are to be seen, sunk in blocks of granite. One of these houses, as already remarked, formed in 1240, and probably at a much earlier time, a bond-mark of the Forest, for there is little doubt that the King's Oven was a building of this kind. We also know that at the same period the stream-work which we now see at the bend of the Wo Brook was in existence, and might even then have been in operation for a considerable time. Called Dryeworke by the Forest perambulators of Richard, Earl of Cornwall, it has not altogether lost the name it bore nearly seven centuries ago.

If the practice was followed on Dartmoor which Carew says was prevalent in Cornwall in his time, it is not difficult to understand the reason that the blowing-houses are always found in such a ruinous condition. That writer says it was customary for the tinners to burn the houses down after they had been in use a few years, in order to obtain the particles of tin that had been carried by the wind into the low thatched roof, and that they usually found sufficient to enable them to build a new house and to give them a substantial surplus. The ingots of tin were probably conveyed from the stream-works to the border towns on the backs of the moorland ponies, or 'small horses,' as they are sometimes called. A woodcut described in 1835 by Mr. Edmund Pearse, surgeon, of Tavistock, as being then very old, exhibited, however, another mode of carrying the metal, but one which we can hardly believe was ever adopted. The picture represented a pack of hounds, harnessed, and laden with small bags of tin, which they were conveying over the moor.

It would appear as though the manorial lords whose rights extended over the purlieus of the Forest sought to interfere in some way with the tinners, for in 1250 King Henry III granted the latter a charter of protection. All knights and others of whom the tinners of Dartmoor held, were enjoined that they should not exact customs and services from them other than they ought, and the liberties granted to them by previous charters were to be maintained. The dues payable on the tin proved a source of considerable revenue, and it is, therefore, not surprising that the King should desire that those who produced the metal should be in no way disturbed. So much wealth was derived from the Stannaries that it is said that Richard, Earl of Cornwall, in whose possession they appear to have been, bought the title of King of the Romans, in 1257, from the profits arising from them. Edward I also recognised the expediency of permitting the tinners to enjoy their rights peacefully. In 1305 he granted a charter for the amendment of the Stannaries both in Cornwall and in Devon, 'and for the tranquillity and advantage of our tinners of the same,' and in this their privileges, which were very important, were set forth and confirmed.

The towns at which all tin found in Devon was to be weighed and stamped were named in the charter, and these are the same as are mentioned in a coinage roll of 1303, namely, Tavistock, Ashburton, and Chagford. The tinners were permitted to sell their tin at those places when stamped, but the King was to retain the right of pre-emption. In 1328 Tavistock ceased to be a Stannary town, and Plympton was created one in its place. The reason assigned for this change was that the distance of Tavistock from the sea made the cost of the carriage of the tin so heavy that traders rarely visited it. However, it regained its old position later, and from the 15th century onward formed one of the four Stannary towns of Devon. Even if the geological evidence was wanting, the situation of these towns would be quite sufficient to show that Dartmoor and its confines formed the sole tin-streaming district of the county.

The tinners of Devon and Cornwall originally formed one body, and were governed by their own peculiar laws, passed at courts, or parliaments, held in the open air. These were of high antiquity, and it has even been supposed that upon them was modelled the legislative assembly of the State. Mr. John Thomas, Vice-Warden of the Stannaries from 1783 to 1812, in a report to the Prince's Council, of the 21st February, 1785, observes that in its constitution the parliament of the tinners was similar to the British. The Lord Warden represented the King; the stannators represented the lords; and the assistants, which were chosen by the stannators, represented the commons. These hypæthral courts were held on Hingston Down, in Cornwall, and there was enacted those laws which probably for a considerable period regulated the mining throughout the two Western Counties. When the tinners of Devon separated from those of Cornwall they established their own parliament at Crockern Tor, on Dartmoor, but when this took place is not known. In the charter of the 9th of Richard I the Stannary of Devon is noticed as being distant from the Stannary of Cornwall, but no reference is made to the tinners' courts. Nor are they mentioned in the charter of Edward I, where, however, the Stannaries are also treated as being distinct from each other. The first record of a parliament held on Crockern Tor is in 1494, but that the tinners assembled there long prior to that date is certain.

When Edward III in 1336 raised the Earldom of Cornwall into a Duchy he bestowed upon his son, the first duke, the Stannaries of Devon and Cornwall, and they have remained an appanage of the Duchy from that time. The Stannary of Devon did not immediately come into the possession of the duke, as it had been granted to Thomas West during his life at a rental of £100 a year, but the King ordered that at the death of the grantee the Stannary should revert to the duke.

In Edward IV's reign the dues from the Stannary of Cornwall fell off, in consequence of the difficulty experienced in supplying the blowing-houses with fuel. To remedy this the King granted a charter in 1466 to the tinners of Cornwall, by which they were to be permitted to take peat from Dartmoor, and this was confirmed by succeeding Sovereigns.

The parliament of 1494 was held on Crockern Tor by authority of Prince Arthur, son of Henry VII, and Duke of Cornwall, and the statutes passed were afterwards printed at the press in the Abbey of Tavistock in 1510. Each of the four Stannary towns sent 24 jurors, as representatives of the tinners of Devon, and among the ordinances passed was one forbidding anyone to possess a tin-work who was the owner of landed property of a value above £10 yearly, unless the work happened to be his by inheritance, or in his own freehold. Another extended these conditions to any abbot, prior, or spiritual person, and a third to various officers of the Stannary and to the foresters of Dartmoor. All who were thus disqualified were liable to a penalty of £20 if they became the owners of tin-works. Other enactments regulated the setting out of bounds of tin-works, and for the marking of tin by the owners of blowing-houses. It was also ordered that no man learned in the law, spiritual or temporal, should be permitted to plead in any Stannary Court, 'nor he a counsell to make bylie.' under a penalty of £20.

Records of other parliaments held on Crockern Tor are extant, and the names of the jurors have been preserved. In 1511 one was held, and others in 1533 and 1534. Later ones, of which we have accounts, were held in the reigns of Edward VI and Elizabeth. One is referred to as having been held on the tor in 1686 in a commission issued a year or two subsequently by James II to John, Earl of Bath, who was then Lord Warden of the Stannaries. The tinners at their parliament had complained to the King that in consequence of a combination of merchants the price of tin had sunk so low as to discourage them in their labours, and prayed that James would take the tin raised in the Stannaries at a fixed rate. The King had been pleased to consent to do so at £3. 10s. 'per cent, Stannary weight,' such being much beyond the current price. The tinners gladly assented to this, and the earl was authorised by the commission to complete the agreement, on behalf of the King and the infant Duke of Cornwall. It is said that the Earl of Bath attended the parliament on the tor accompanied by a retinue of three hundred gentlemen well mounted. In a precept from the Vice-Warden of the Stannaries, the Hon. Samuel Rolle, to the Stannators of Plympton, dated 25th August, 1703, it is set forth that a parliament had been appointed to assemble at Crockern Tor, on the 23rd September following, at 8-o'clock in the morning. If it were now the custom for legislative councils to meet under similar conditions it is just possible that a lack of candidates for membership might be experienced.

Though during this later period the tinners had continued to regulate all matters pertaining to the Stannary, their power had been gradually waning. Its decline may be traced from the 16th century, when their treatment of Richard Strode caused it to be viewed with concern. Strode was thrown into the Stannary prison at Lydford Castle in default of payment of a fine inflicted by the tinners in consequence of his action in bringing in a bill in the Imperial Parliament to restrain them from filling the streams of Dartmoor with sand, whereby the navigation of the havens had been seriously affected. He was delivered from his prison by a writ of privilege, and subsequently procured an Act for his protection. In this passage-at-arms between Westminster and Crockern Tor the latter proved to be the weaker.

A parliament is said to have been held on the tor as late as 1749, and Bellamy, in his *Thousand Facts*, states that even this was not the last. But for some time it had been customary for the tinners merely to meet on the hill on the moor, and to adjourn their court to Tavistock.

If, as some have supposed, Crockern Tor was the seat of an ancient British court of judicature, we should probably be correct in regarding the tinners' parliament as a survival of that earlier assembly, and be led to the belief that the tinners of Devon met there even when they formed one body with those of the sister county. But though this may be probable, it seems more so that there were no gatherings of miners on the tor until the Devon tinners became a distinct Corporation. Still, this does not rob it of its romantic associations. Its known history is sufficient to endow it with an interest such as no other hill on Dartmoor possesses, and its sight will always serve to turn the thoughts back to those times when the hardy Stannators, in defiance of the elements, flocked thither at their Warden's call. These recollections will arise, although the spoiler has visited the tor and removed the visible signs of the rude court. The grey rocks that crown the hill are mute, but as one stands beside them there rises to the recollection the story of 'deserted Crockern.'

Crockern Tor

*****

VII

THE REEVES AND THE FORESTERS.

When Dartmoor on being severed from the Crown ceased to be a Forest in law, and became a chase, it lost some of its privileges, but none of its value as a hunting ground. Its princely owners possessed the right of still preserving the deer, and that this was done the many allusions to them in its records testify. Foresters were appointed, as heretofore, to enforce the laws made for their protection, and offenders against these were brought before the court at Lydford. These officers had also other duties, among which were the collection of certain rents, and fees for the folding of cattle and the cutting of peat, and these grew in importance as the resources of the Forest, or chase, became more fully developed.

The account rendered by the officers who had charge of the moor was separate from that of the manor of Lydford. Certain of the profits arising from the former were, however, omitted in the return relating to it, and were included in the account of the manor. This seems to shew that, although the two were treated as being distinct, they were yet regarded as having some sort of connection. It does not appear likely that the Forest was waste of the manor. As we have already seen , it is not certain that there was a manor of Lydford before the 13th century, and when, 12 years after we first hear of it, it is mentioned in the Charter of Henry III, it is in such a manner as to preclude the supposition that the Forest formed part of it. The King granted to his brother the manor of Lydford and all its appurtenances. If the Forest belonged to it there would have been no need to mention it at all; the word 'appurtenances' would include it. But the Charter proceeds: 'Together with the Forest of Dartmoor and all the appurtenances of the same Forest,' and these words are also employed in grants of a later date. We can therefore scarcely come to any other conclusion than that the manor and Forest were two separate possessions. The connection which existed between them, and which it is likely had an early origin, was not improbably due to the fact that they were in the hands of one owner. As time went on, and one court exercised jurisdiction over both, this connection would become closer, and it is not difficult to see that certain of the profits of the Forest, that is, such as were not derived from the pasturage and turbary, might at length be regarded as belonging to the manor. Thus we find that a certain village in the Forest (probably Babeney and Pizwell), and which in 1300 rendered 110s. 4d. yearly, was said to pertain to the manor of Lydford; but the record in which this occurs does not state that the turbary and pasturage, which are named as being then worth £40 yearly, belonged to the manor. No mention of the latter is made in connection with them; the sum they yielded is returned as being the profit of the Forest of Dartmoor.

The accounts of the officers of the manor and Forest in which the sources of revenue and the nature of the disbursements are shewn, throw considerable light on the customs of the moor. We learn something of the number of the beasts agisted, and also what kind they were; of the peat-cutting industry; of new enclosures, of the fines, or rents, of the vils, besides many other matters, and also what officers were employed. In the Close Rolls of the 3rd and 7th of Henry III there are writs commanding the election of verderers, but after the grant of the Forest to the Earl of Cornwall we find only bailiffs or reeves, and foresters and priours. The Earl's bailiff was Ralph de Cheverston, who seems to have been influenced by a desire to obtain an increased revenue from the moor, for he is reported in 1275 by the jurors of the Hundred of Plympton and the Borough of Okehampton, to have doubled the agistment fees, demanding 1d. for an ox, and 2d. for a horse. Twenty years later the fee for each head of cattle was 1½d., so that there was a still further advance, but the fee for the grazing of horses remained the same. At this time one officer returned the receipts and expenses of both the manor and the moor, but subsequently the duties were divided. An account of the Duchy possessions in 1342, the year in which they came into the hands of Prince Edward, shews that there were then three officers – the reeve of the Borough of Lydford, the reeve of Dartmoor, and the receiver of the profits of the agistments on the moor, of the peat, and of the venville rents.

There are numerous entries relating to the peat, or coal, as it was termed, in the returns of the profits of the moor. In 1296 we find that twenty-seven cutters and preparers of the fuel returned 11s. 3d., being 5d. from each one; in the Inquisition taken after Earl Edmund's death, in 1300, the 'sale of coals' is mentioned as forming part of the profits arising from the moor; and in 1358 'the turbary of coals' is named in John Dabernan's account. The cutting of peat, and the making of coals on the moor, formed one of the subjects considered at an Inquisition taken at Lydford in 1382. Early in the 17th century it was suggested in a letter to the Earl of Salisbury that James I should exact tithe of the value of the peat yearly cut on the moor, and which was stated to be 100,000 horse loads. Charles I in 1626 let the Forest to Sir Thomas Reynell for 31 years, and in the lease is named among the appurtenances of the moor 'the chieftage, or head silver, of certain coal men for licence of digging turves there.'

The amount returned in 1296 for the pannage of pigs was 2s. 3d. As there were no trees on the moor, there could, of course, have been no mast for the animals, and it is, therefore, probable that they were merely turned into the border coppices. Swine were permitted to run in Forests from 15 days prior to

Michaelmas until 40 days after, but it would appear that only certain persons had a right to turn them on Dartmoor. The Jury of Survey, in making their presentment, in 1609, say that no stranger, that is no one who is not a Dartmoor Commoner, ought to put any sheep or pigs in the Forest. They further say that such strangers as have done so, and whose pigs 'have subverted and spoyled the soyle of this said Forest,' have usually been summoned to Lydford and fined.

Among what were called the perquisites of the courts were fines for trespass, for making default, for false claims, for turning cattle or horses on the Forest without having caused them to be entered on the agistment roll, and for taking dogs there at seasons when they were not allowed within its bounds.

The disbursements shown on the accounts include 60s. to the rector of Lydford; this was the tithe of the herbage of the moor, and was granted the Church of St. Petrock by Henry III, in 1236; the wages and food of the foresters, and of the herdsmen who attended to the cattle agisted on the moor, and the costs of repairs to certain houses there.

In later returns we find among the profits arising from the Forest sums of money for small parcels of land newly enclosed. Thus in 1347 John Robert pays 3d. for two acres of waste near the Dart, and William Dunbrigge (a farm of Dunnabridge) pays 6d. for four acres near the Cherry Brook. In 1354 4d. is received from John Frensse (French) for a piece of land taken by him at Pizwell; and in 1362 Abraham Eliot is credited with 6d. for two acres at Dunnabridge Ford, and a piece of land at Sherburton. Robert Salton also pays 1$^1/_2$d. for half an acre at Pollerds Well, and John Northmore a like sum for one acre at Lether Tor. These small enclosures are numerous, and except in a few instances their names can be identified. An examination of them, something of their history being known, is by no means devoid of interest. When we can look upon an old drift pound and remember that the reeve of Dartmoor nearly 600 years ago paid 3d. for a lock to its gate: when we can call to mind the names of the men who in that day built the rude walls near it, now so grey and lichen-stained: and when the Forest story tells us that the clerk who wrote out the lists of the agistments on the moor, and was fined 6s. 8d. for his pains, also helped to number the beasts, and that such as were not claimed at a certain time were driven to this pound, and that it is used for the same purpose today, we can feel that there is yet a link connecting us with the Dartmoor of the past.

There are also returns in the accounts of the moor for the 'predas,' or pasturage grounds, and for cattle agisted outside the Forest. This payment to the Prince serves as a further proof that he possessed rights not only over the Forest, but over its purlieus as well. Money was also received, among other sources, from the sale of estrays, and as rent from 'tynsmyths,' which seems to have been the payments for the small enclosures near the blowing-houses of the tinners.

Certain expenses were incurred for driving the moor to ascertain the number of beasts pastured thereon, and for making proclamation of the agistments. In one account there is a charge of 12d. for parchment for the Court Rolls and other necessary things, and credit is taken for 6d. paid to the clerk for writing out the account. The duties of this officer took him all round the moor, for he had to visit the various places on its confines in order to ascertain the number of beasts that were to be agisted, in order that he might enter them on his list.

The food of the foresters and the herdsmen was sometimes provided. In 1300 there is a charge of 62s., being the stipend of six foresters, and 66s. 6d. for the food and wages of twelve herdsmen, for attending to the cattle agisted on the moor from May until August. Another entry 8 or 9 years later shows a payment of 42s. for the wages and keep of six foresters, and of 51s. for the wages and expenses of eight herdsmen. In 1344 six foresters are each paid 8s. 8d., credit being taken for 52s. In addition to these charges there are also sums entered as having been paid to the foresters for expenses.

There is an interesting account rendered in the 18th of Henry VII, which enables us to obtain a good view of the receipts and disbursements of the reeves and foresters. The reeve of the Borough of Lydford returns £4. 3s., arising from the following: – Rents of freeholders, rents from lands and tenements outside the borough, a customary payment called 'Foldepeny,' rent for the pasture round the castle, farm of the mill, tolls of the fair, and perquisites of courts. Out of this he pays the rector's tithe of £3, showing his clear receipts to amount to £1. 3s. The reeve of the manor of Lydford returns £9. 15s. 1d., being rents for small parcels of waste land on the moor, the farm of the mill there, and mort gabel. The forester of the east quarter of the Forest makes a return of £18. 15s. 7½d., the amount being made up by the rents of the vils bordering his quarter, and the fees for agistments within it, together with the customary payments from the peat-cutters, and from persons trespassing with their cattle, the payments from the censers, and the perquisites of courts. From the total sum he deducts the wages of two foresters, a herdsman, and the clerk. The return of the foresters of the west, south, and north quarters, are very similar; the total receipts of the first being £9. 12s. 2d.; of the second, £17. 8s. 10¾d.; and of the last £13. 14s. 0½d.; and from these amounts the disbursements are deducted.

There is still a reeve of the Forest, and there are priours, or, as we now call them, moormen, but the foresters are seen no longer. But though many of the old customs have departed, Dartmoor is still reminiscent of them, and herein lies one of its potent charms.

VIII

THE CHASE OF OKEHAMPTON

William the Conqueror, when he shared with his followers the lands they had helped him to gain, was able, with no sacrifice to himself, to be doubly mindful of those whom he particularly desired to reward, and any among his adherents who could claim relationship with him doubtless came within that category. When Saxon thanes were in some instances supplanted by 'ignoble grooms, the scum of armies,' it is just possible that in that age, whatever may be the case in the present day, patronage was distributed with little regard to the fitness of individuals for the posts conferred upon them. It is impossible to determine whether the Norman knight who was invested with the hereditary shrievalty of Devon, the command of the Castle of Exeter, and upon whom was also bestowed the honour of Okehampton, was, or was not, possessed of those administrative abilities which such an important position demanded. This follower of the Conqueror was Baldwin de Brionys, who, like William himself, was descended with the bend sinister from Richard, father of Robert the Devil. He held the great barony of Okehampton in fief under the Crown, on the tenure of ninety-two knights' service, and is said to have built the Castle on the outskirts of the town. But the foundations of by far the greater part of the walls that now, hoary and crumbling, partially hide themselves amid the trees that clothe the side of the hill which was chosen as the site of the fortress, were laid at a time much later than that of the powerful feudal lord.

With this family, upon which was afterwards bestowed the Earldom of Devon, the Courtenays became allied by marriage in the 13th century, and after the death of the Countess, Isabella de Fortibus, in 1292, succeeded to the title. The barony of Okehampton continued in that line until 1556, and the earldom to our own time, but both with intervals of forfeiture.

The ancient name of the town which formed the head of the barony was Ockmenton, which it derived from the two Dartmoor streams immediately above the confluence of which it is placed. These are the East and the West Ockment, or, as the name is sometimes rendered, and possibly more correctly, Okement. The former rises in a hollow known as Skit Bottom, about 3½ miles southward of Halstock, and the latter has its source in a wild part of the moor very near to the northern bank of Cranmere Pool. The name is traceable to a

Celtic root, 'osc,' signifying 'water,' and is found in several objects near these two streams, and also in other parts of the moor. On the ridge to the east of the upper waters of the East Ockment we have Ock, or Oke Tor; between the streams is Ockment Hill; and south-westward of a small feeder of the West Ockment, and which joins it below Kneeset Foot, we have the hill known as Watern Oke. We also find the word in the Ockery, near Princetown, and in Water Oke Corner, in the south of the moor.

The commons belonging to the parish, and abutting on the Forest of Dartmoor, formed part of a chase which included within its limits a considerable tract of country towards the north, a line drawn from Dunsland Cross to Stow Bridge, near Exbourne, marking the boundary in that direction. Within this chase was a park, lying to the south of the town and the castle, and many of its ancient oaks and hollies yet dot the slopes that rise moorward from the river. This extensive range of hill and dale, the hunting ground of the lords of Okehampton, continued to be an appanage of the barony for nearly five centuries, its last possessor being Henry Courtenay, who was created Marquis of Exeter by Henry VIII, and by him also consigned to the headsman.

This earl was the son of William Courtenay and Katherine, youngest daughter of Edward IV. During the earlier part of his career he was greatly in favour with Henry VIII, and at the Field of the Cloth of Gold broke a lance against the French King. He was Lord Warden of the Stannaries, and at two of the Tinners' Parliaments held at Crockern Tor in this reign, of which we have an account, was represented by Sir Philip Champernowne. In 1538 he was accused of having held correspondence with Cardinal Pole, who was intriguing against Henry, and was attainted and beheaded, all his honours being forfeited.

In the 24th of Henry VIII, six years before the Marquis fell into disgrace, an inquiry was held relative to the Chase of Okehampton, and a return of the boundaries made by the commissioners. This return is particularly interesting. It shows the line of demarcation between the Forest and the commons in 1532, and it can scarcely be doubted that the boundary as recognised then as belonging equally to the lords of Okehampton and the lords of the Forest, was the same as that perambulated in 1240. The Forest bounds in this part of the moor were not clearly set forth by the perambulators of that early time, and anything that helps us to determine where the line ran is of value. Nothing is more certain than that the boundary of this part of the chase was conterminous with that of the Forest, consequently the objects mentioned in the return made by the commissioners as here defining the limits of the one, would also show the limits of the other. The return, if not perfectly conclusive, goes very far to prove that the perambulators of Richard, Earl of Cornwall, on reaching the West Ockment, made their way to the summit of the hill we now call High Willes, and thence by West Mil Tor and Row Tor to St. Michael's Chapel of Halstock.

In the return the first of these objects is given as Hight Wyll, but the names of the others have undergone no change. The direction in which the boundary-line of the chase is traced across the commons is the reverse of that followed by the Forest perambulators, so that the names occur in an opposite order to that here given. Preceding St. Michael's Chapel, but following it, if we trace the footsteps of the perambulators, is a bond-mark set down in the commissioners' return as Netelham Stappys, or Steps. This, although the name is now lost, there cannot be a doubt, is the crossing-place on the East Ockment called Chapel Ford. Thus we shall scarcely fail to be convinced that the line of the ancient Forest as it ran from the West to the East Ockment passed over the three tors which appear as though designed by Nature to mark its limits.

Among some marginal notes, made chiefly by the Rev. H. G. Fothergill, a former rector of Belstone, in a copy of a work on Okehampton, by William B. Bridges, published in parts about the year 1839, is one giving the boundary of the Okehampton Commons. It is evidently an extract, and, judging from its style, of a date which even at that time was not a recent one. The boundary-line is very clearly drawn, and is practically the same as that set forth by the commissioners of the Marquis of Exeter, in 1532. The three tors are named, and the line is said to pass over their summits.

More than once during its history has the barony of Okehampton escheated to the Crown, on the attainder of its noble possessor. Some of the lands would also appear to have been in the hands of the King, or of the Earl of Cornwall, after the death of Lord Hugh Courtenay, in 1291, if by certain pasturage mentioned in a return of the profits of the moor in 1296, the grazing-ground within the Park of Okehampton is intended. The account in question is that of the ministers of Earl Edmund, and one of the items of profit returned under the heading 'Dartmoor,' is £1. 13s. 3d., for 399 cattle at a farm near Okehampton. In 1300, in an account rendered to the Crown by John de Tresympel, under the same heading the 'pasture next Okehampton' is again mentioned, but no profit is shown because no cattle came there. This pasturage, the sum received for which is kept separate from the agistment fees, certainly seems to have been an enclosed tract, and if so it is difficult to see that it was any other than the Park. When William of Worcester passed through Okehampton the barony also appears to have been in the hands of the King, since the castle is spoken of by him as a Royal fortress.

Although the extensive Chase of Okehampton belonged to the Marquis of Exeter, the park did not form a portion of his domain. At all events, this appears to have been the case, for in a letter of Queen Catherine, of the 18th of Henry VIII, it is mentioned as though it were a Royal possession. The letter is addressed by the Queen to 'owre trusty and welbeloved sarvant, Robert Cruewis, keeper of owre Parke of Okehampton,' and he is commanded upon sight of it to deliver to the bearer 'one buck of season, to be taken as of our gyfte owte of owre parke in Ockhampton.' It is probable that on the lands of the barony being restored after one of the forfeitures, the park was excepted and retained by the King.

On the attainder of the Marquis of Exeter, his son, Edward Courtenay, was committed to the Tower, although not charged with any crime. He was restored to liberty by Mary, who admitted him to her favour, and he soon after received the title of the Earl of Devon. At an inquisition taken after his death, which occurred at Padua, his heirs were found to be members of the families of Trethurffe, Arundle, Mohun, and Trelawny, and to them passed what remained of the possessions of the ancient house. The Earldom of Devon became extinct, though it has since been revived.

But the extensive lands of the barony and its dependencies had become reduced to a shade of what they once were. Soon after the execution of the Marquis of Exeter, Henry VIII had laid Okehampton Castle in ruins, and seized upon the lands there. At the suggestion of Richard Pollard he disparked the noble hunting-ground, and destroyed most of the game, with the intention of turning the land to agricultural purposes. But the project did not succeed, and the King was obliged to forego the profit he had hoped would accrue from it. It is said that many complaints reached Henry, and that Richard Pollard lost the King's favour. Dartmoor was true to its traditions, and the man who sought to attack it got the worst of the bargain. If the record is correct, he never smiled afterwards.

The park is situated at the northern extremity of the hill, which terminates in the valley through which the two Ockments flow to meet each other. The part of it nearest this valley is by far the most interesting, for there remain vestiges of its former sylvan honours. Across the valley the venerable ruins of the castle are seen embosomed in foliage, almost the only visible sign of the former presence here of the powerful house founded by De Brionys. Like the line of those who were once its lords, it has witnessed many changes of fortune. But through all time was kinder to it than man. He who 'turned the cowls adrift,' accomplished by an act of 'senseless barbarism' what the years would have failed yet to effect. Indeed, they have, in great measure, repaired the injury he wrought. For time by its touch has silently moulded the shattered stronghold into a thing of beauty.

Okehampton Castle

*****

IX

THE WASTE OF SIR WILLIAM PETRE

At the Dissolution a change took place in the ownership of more than one of the commons in the precincts of the Forest of Dartmoor. Much of that great tract of land in the southern part of the moor, extending from the Dart to the Tavy, and which the monks had long enjoyed, was taken from them, and disposed of to private individuals. And probably on very easy terms. What had cost nothing could, of course, be sold at a low price; as Fuller quaintly remarks, 'cheap pennyworths were at that time obtained out of the land of the church.'

Whatever view the Commoners of Devon may have taken of the causes which led to the monks being despoiled of their possessions, it is probable that they were not particularly sorry when they ceased to hold any manorial rights on the moor. On several occasions the abbots had claimed powers which did not belong to them, and had shown themselves unmindful of everything but their own interests. We have seen how the abbots of Buckland, the holders of Walkhampton and Sheepstor commons, laid certain claims with respect to the wastes, and also how the abbots of Buckfast, within the limits of whose manors lay the commons of Holne, Buckfastleigh, and Brent, did the same, and, in the words of the jurors of the Hundred of Stanborough, 'to the injury of all the country.' More than one circumstance tends to show that great as were the possessions of the monks of Buckfast they were not at all averse to adding to them, even though by so doing they encroached upon the rights of others. Unless the boundary line in the neighbourhood of Eastern Whitaburrow, and which we shall presently notice, was altered by them, it is difficult to see by whom the change was first made.

The old map of Dartmoor in the Albert Memorial Museum, at Exeter, before referred to, seems to have been made with special regard to Brent Moor, much more space being devoted to it than to any other part of the waste. The map is not drawn to scale, in fact it is fanciful in design, the Forest being represented by a circle, and the names of most of the few places mentioned painted on labels or scrolls. But the relative situations of the objects shewn are nevertheless correct. Brent Moor occupies the centre of the map, and the boundary line between it and Ugborough Moor is plainly set out. From these circumstances it has been considered probable that the map was prepared in relation to some dispute as to this boundary. If the supposition be correct it would appear that the Abbot of Buckfast was embroiled in the 15th century (for the map is regarded as being of that date) with his neighbours on the south-west, the men of the 'vill of Ugbirough.' The writing on the map shows it to be of the middle or latter part of the 15th century, and hence the dispute, if the map really was prepared in connection with one, cannot be that which is referred to later as having taken place in the time of Henry V. This later action was in respect of an agistment, but a map may have been produced, nevertheless, for in the reference to the case it is mentioned that an admission was made that between the Forest and the abbots' moors 'only well-known marks, and bounds, and writings of perambulation' existed. To show these bounds a map may therefore have been prepared. But apart from the evidently later date of the map, it can hardly have any connection with the case tried in Henry V's time, for if so equal prominence would have been given to the three moors possessed by the abbots. But it is Brent Moor and the adjoining Ugborough Moor that have received the most attention from the draughtsman, and that it was prepared for the purpose of showing the boundary between those two commons there is little doubt.

The abbots of Buckfast appear to have regarded the moors within their manors as their freehold, in fact, they were claimed to be so by one of them in a letter to Henry, Marquis of Exeter, and to the rest of the King's Council. This abbot was John Rede, who, in Henry VIII's reign, laid claim to the three moors as parcels of his manors. The Commoners of Devon disputed his claim, and the abbot was indicted at the court at Lydford. He then addressed himself to the Marquis of Exeter, and complained that the foresters had driven his moors, notwithstanding that they were his freehold. The abbot concludes his letter with the assurance that he '& his seid covent dayly hath doon & so shall contynue ther dayly prayors to God for yor psperous contynuans longe to endure.' Unfortunately for the abbot, Bluff King Hal did not permit the brothers of Our Lady of Buckfast to fulfil this promise. Ere long they were expelled from their secluded home on the banks of the beautiful Dart, and it needed no law of Lydford to settle their differences with the commoners.

When the possessions of the religious houses were diverted from the purposes intended by their donors, and were bargained for like ordinary property, those who were in favour in high places did not neglect the opportunity afforded them of enriching themselves. Sir Thomas Dennys purchased the manor of Buckfast, and seems also to have claimed the whole of the moors over which the abbots had exercised rights. In this instance the commoners certainly did not benefit by the exchange, of a Churchman for a knight as a manorial lord. If the abbot had shown himself rapacious Sir Thomas Dennys was not outdone by him. In 1541 a dispute arose between him and the inhabitants of Buckfastleigh as to the rights of the venville tenants on the moors of Holne, Buckfastleigh, and Brent. On the matter being carried before the King in Council it was ordered that the venville men and other border tenants were to continue to enjoy those rights on the commons to which they had hitherto been accustomed, until the Council, after receiving the report of certain commissioners, appointed to inquire into the matter, might order otherwise. There is a document in existence setting forth the rights, and also stating the grievances of the commoners, which has been supposed to relate to this commission. In it the action of the abbot, John Rede, in claiming the commons, is styled his 'fals craft and dowyngs,' and Sir Thomas Dennys, who is stated in the instrument to have purchased the abbot's demesnes, is accused of using 'subtyll and crafty meanys.' The estates are said to have been valued at £14 a year, but that since they had come into the possession of Sir Thomas he had made £52. 15s. a year of them. Sir Thomas evidently drove a good bargain, though it is certain that he never succeeded in his claims in relation to the moorland portions of his manor, and which would have deprived the venville men of their rights. These they have always been able to maintain, despite the vexatious suits of 'holy friar,' or 'knight of the shire.'

The manor of South Brent was purchased at the Dissolution by Sir William Petre. The moor which then belonged to it is of considerable size, extending from in the in-ground to the Forest, and from the Avon on the east to the summit of the ridge between that stream and the Erme on the west. Unlike Sir Thomas Dennys, we do not find that Sir William Petre sought to interfere with the rights of the Commoners of Devon. A man who could so accommodate himself to circumstances as to serve under four such monarchs as Henry VIII, Edward VI, Mary, and Elizabeth, would not be likely to get involved in a dispute about agistment fees, particularly if he saw such would probably result in a victory for his opponents, and also cause him to grow unpopular. We can more easily imagine him to be content with the cultivated and valuable part of his manor, and, satisfied that his own rights on the commons were not infringed, and that no encroachments were made by the holders of adjoining lands, to be willing to allow the commoners to quietly enjoy what they claimed as their own. He was a native of Devonshire, and probably knew of what rights on Dartmoor the men of the county were entitled, and how they were always ready to guard them.

Sir William was the son of John Petre, of Tor Brian, but whether he was born in that parish is not certain, some accounts stating that this occurred at Exeter. He was educated at Exeter College, Oxford, afterwards removing to All Souls, of which he was elected fellow in 1523. In 1526 he took the degree of Bachelor of Civil Law, and 6 years later that of Doctor of the same faculty. Having, while acting in the capacity of tutor to the Earl of Wiltshire's son, attracted the notice of Thomas Cromwell, who was in favour with Henry VIII, he was introduced at Court. Step by step he rose, and in 1543 was appointed Secretary of State. This office he also held under the three succeeding rulers, standing high in favour of each. So skilful was he in adapting his conduct to the changes of Government that he gained their confidence, and was thus able to retain, when Popery was restored by Mary, the valuable estates he had acquired from the spoliation of the religious houses in the time of Henry VIII, and was afterwards able to ingratiate himself with Elizabeth. He died in 1571, leaving seven manors in Devonshire, besides others in several counties.

On the 25th August, 1557, an Inquisition was taken at Brent relative to the bounds of Brent Moor. Three weeks previously a commission had been issued to Sir Thomas Dennys and others to survey the bounds between the Forest and the common, and in the meantime this had been done. It is evident that in this part of their moors the abbots of Buckfast had encroached upon the Forest, for in their return the jurors give as the boundary line between it and Brent Moor an entirely different one to that named by the perambulators of 1240. We have already seen that the Forest boundary ran from the confluence of the Wellabrook and the Avon to a cairn known as Eastern Whitaburrow, and thence to Western Whitaburrow, which line would include within the Forest a sloping tract of land called Bishop's Mead, or, in the Devonshire vernacular, Bush Meads. It is interesting to note that the latter form of the name was in use 350 years ago, for the jurors refer to the place as 'Bishop's Mead, otherwise Busshe Mead.' The line laid down by the jurors runs from Western Whitaburrow to Buckland Ford, and thence to the Avon, which it follows to its confluence with the Wellabrook, thus throwing the whole of Bishop's Mead and Eastern Whitaburrow outside the Forest, and claiming them as part of Brent Moor. As it is only reasonable to suppose that the jurors followed the line that was regarded in the neighbourhood as being the true one, and did not lay down a fresh boundary, we can only conclude that Bishop's Mead and Eastern Whitaburrow had been claimed as being part of Brent Moor by the abbots of Buckfast. That the Brent commoners, however, were not averse to the claim, we can readily believe, and hence would show no desire to interfere with the four stone crosses which the jury certified that they had erected on the boundary line, especially as one of them marked that part of their common where the encroachment on the Forest had been made. But the fact of the abbots having set up a claim to this tract of land, and the erection of bond-marks by the jury of the survey of 1557, of course, gave them no title to it, and, as we have before observed, the jurors who perambulated the Forest boundary in 1609 took no notice of it, but continued on their way from the Wellabrook to Eastern Whitaburrow, as their predecessors had done. In 1786 a court was held at Lydford Castle to inquire, among other matters, as to the bounds of the Forest, and in their presentment they also return Eastern Whitaburrow as a boundary.

Of the four crosses said to have been set up by the jurors, one, and probably two, were in existence before the time of their survey. The first was on Three Barrows, and marked the boundary between the moors of Brent and Ugborough. A cross is shewn there on the old map in the Museum at Exeter, and is named Hobajohn's Cross, and there is little doubt that this was one referred to by the jurors. They probably found it prostrate on the hill and set it up when making their survey. The next was on Western Whitaburrow, and to that the name of the holder of the moor became attached, for the spot is known as Petre's Cross to this day. The third was at Buckland Ford, and the fourth, Huntingdon Cross, still stands at the confluence of the Avon and the Wellabrook. As the latter is on the line of the Monk's Path across the Forest, the Abbots' Way, there is not much doubt that, like Hobajohn's Cross, it was erected long before the jurors of 1557 visited the moor. The cross at Western Whitaburrow, and that at Buckland Ford, may have been set up for the first time when the survey was made.

The spoliator has, unfortunately, been at work among these relics. Huntingdon Cross is happily uninjured, but of Hobajohn's Cross the shattered head alone remains. Petre's Cross was intact until about the middle of the last century, when it was destroyed by some workmen. The cross at Buckland Ford has disappeared. We have frequently searched for it, but without success. Beyond the reference to it in the jurors' return there is no mention of it anywhere, nor could we ever learn of anyone who had seen it.

We have spoken of two boundary stones on the summit of Ryder's Hill, between Holne and Buckfastleigh Moors. One of these is much older looking than the other, and is only about 2 feet high. It is known as Petre's Boundstone, or more generally as Petre-on-the-Mount, a name which points to some connection with the manorial lord of Brent. The example set by the abbots of Buckfast and the commoners of Brent was followed by the commoners, or the lords of the manors, of Ugborough and Ermington. The bounds of these moors are also thrust out into the Forest, and this had occurred, at all events, in the case of the latter, so early as 1603. It was in all probability this fact that caused the Forest perambulators of 1609 to be so explicit in naming the boundary line, as it ran from Western Whitaburrow to the River Erme.

The manor of Brent continued in the family of Petre through several descents, but at the end of the 18th century most of the Devonshire estates were sold. The manor has since been dismembered, and Brent Moor no longer forms a part of it. It was once a great possession, and in early times the Abbot of Buckfast there held undisputed sway. Now its importance has become entirely a thing of the past.

> 'For of its great name I wis
> It only now the shadow is.'

Petre-on-the-Mount, Ryder's Hill

*****

X

SUNDAY, THE 21ST OCTOBER 1638

Those who in early days slowly made their way up the valley of the Dart, seeking to subdue Nature, and to wrest from her land for tillage and for pasture, on reaching the confines of the moor found there another stream, that lost itself in the larger, and invited them to turn aside and trace it to its birthplace. This was the Webburn, and those who passed up its banks saw that soon it branched, and that the arms led far up among the hills. But the valleys through which these streams coursed were sheltered, nevertheless, the eastern one being particularly so. On one side a huge ridge, and on the other a range of tors, shielded it from the blasts, while to the south it was open. These happy conditions enabled the husbandman to raise his crops and the herdsman to feed his cattle in the crofts which he had formed, and the vale of Widecombe looked like a garden in a desert. Then were some attracted to the valley down which came the other branch of the stream, and which lay on the further side of the great ridge. Others desired to penetrate yet deeper into the moor, and the Dart became their guide, leading them to a region where they saw that Nature had put off her vestures of green and donned a sombre garb.

That the medieval settlers in the Forest of Dartmoor pushed their way into it from the neighbourhood of Widecombe and Holne there can be no doubt. Their farms are found only in that part of the Forest on which those parishes abut, and in every instance on the banks of the two branches of the Dart or their tributaries. On none of the other streams of the moor do similar ancient farms exist; it was through the valley of the Dart alone that the rude cultivation of a former time was carried into the Forest.

The dwellers in these farms, although the latter were situated within the parish of Lydford, naturally felt less attached to that place, from which they were separated by many miles of wild moor, than to Widecombe, to which most of them were comparatively near. The former it is not likely they ever visited, except when business connected with the courts of the Forest took them there, but with regard to Widecombe it was different. They worshipped at that church, and in 1260, when we first hear of them, were permitted by the Bishop of Exeter to pay certain of their tithes there, instead of to their parish church of Lydford. And not only in the matter of tithes do these Forest men seem to have been connected with Widecombe. When Thomas Bernaford, the

Widecombe Church

Lydford Church

rector of Lydford, in 1702 filed a bill in the Exchequer against John Hext and others, claiming tithes from the holders of the ancient farms, it is stated in reply that they pay them to the rector of Widecombe, and it was also deposed that when any of them had been summoned they had appeared before the justices of the division in which Widecombe is situated, and not before those of Lydford. In the notes to Carrington's poem of *Dartmoor*, it is also stated that from the first existence of poor-rates, all the east quarter of the moor, which is that part of it in which the greater number of the ancient Forest farms are situated, paid their rates at Widecombe, and continued to do so until 1815. There can be little doubt that the dwellers on these farms, although free tenants of the Forest of Dartmoor, did not regard themselves as being Lydford men, but rather as belonging to Widecombe. Lydford was the real head of the Forest, and Widecombe had no official connection with it, but it was, nevertheless, the latter place that possessed the greater interest for the Forest men, and to which they resorted. It does not, of course, figure in the records of the Lydford courts, but during several centuries it must have played a far more important part in the history of the moorland dwellers, than the administrative centre of the Forest ever did.

The absence of any direct roads from Lydford village to the eastern borders of the Forest, and the distance from one to the other were no doubt important reasons why there was so little communication between the inhabitants of the two districts. Another is to be found in the fact that the Forest dwellers were certainly not originally natives of Lydford, but, as we have said, were in all probability the descendants of settlers who found their way into the waste from the valleys round Widecombe and Holne. Yet it is likely that the old dwellers in the south-eastern corner of Dartmoor knew more about the village of Lydford than do those who live upon the ancient holdings today. Certain services had then to be performed which necessitated the attendance of the Forest tenants at the courts held there. When these became things of the past there was no longer any cause for journeying thither, and having little or no curiosity about the place, they did not trouble to visit it. We have known men who have grown grey in the Forest, and who have never seen Lydford village, nor even been within many miles of it; and, on the other hand, we are acquainted with Lydford men who are utter strangers to any part of Dartmoor except that adjacent to their home. The wild hills of the moor, though possessing an attraction for many of us, do not tempt all, and there are those among the borderers who would not give themselves the trouble to cross them without a strong reason.

The parish of Widecombe is conterminous with the Forest for a distance of about 4 miles, extending from a point just above the homesteads of Pizwell to Dartmeet. Its cultivated portions lie mainly in the valleys watered by the branches of the Webburn, which thrust themselves far up among the hills; all its more elevated parts consist of moorland. The village of Widecombe, which is 3 miles outside the Forest boundary, is charmingly placed at about the middle of the valley of the East Webburn, or Niprell, as the stream was anciently called. Viewed from the commons on the east, its situation will be best appreciated. There it will be seen that the valley widens just where the village stands, to contract again a short distance below it. In the combes formed by the retreating sides are fields, and a few farmsteads nestling in some unusually well-sheltered spot. In the centre the ground rises slightly, and there, amid the trees, are seen the roofs of the few houses that constitute the village, and the fine tower of the ancient church. The western side of the valley is formed by the lofty ridge of Hameldon and the downs that extend southward from it; the eastern by the slopes of Blackslade Down and Widecombe Hill; and towards its head by a range of three fine tors – Bonehill Rocks, Chinkwell, and Honeybag. These overlook the narrower part of the vale, and form a fine background to the view when the village is approached from the south.

At Widecombe was anciently seated the family of Fitz-Ralph, of which, it is said, Richard Fitz-Ralph, who, in the 14th century was Primate of Ireland, was a member. It has sometimes been stated that he was born here, but though he is known to have been a Devonshire man, there appears to be some doubt as to whether Widecombe can claim the honour of being his birthplace. Of North Hall, the dwelling of the Fitz-Ralphs, nothing is now to be seen; a few grassy mounds alone show where it stood. But, fortunately, a description of it has been handed down to us by one who dwelt at Widecombe in the first half of the 17th century. Its glories had then long departed, and the chronicler tells us that the goodly mansion was much decayed, but sufficient remained of it to show what it once had been, and tradition had preserved an account of its former state.

Seated in this pleasant vale, hidden away among the tors and removed from all frequented paths, there was little to disturb the serenity of the moorland village. Children grew up in the shadow of the hills crested with the granite piles, and found their avocations there, when as youths and maidens they were taught to labour. Young men took to themselves wives from the peaceful vale, and the same church that had witnessed the union of their parents blessed their own. There the noontide of their lives was spent, and there the evening shadows fell. In the quiet churchyard where their grandsires lay, they found at length a resting-place, and the tolling of the bell in the old tower, to which they had so often listened, fell upon the ears of children whose lives were to be the counterpart of the one then ended.

But the wonted tranquillity of the vale of Widecombe was rudely disturbed one autumn Sabbath. The accustomed rural sounds were drowned in the roar of the storm, and in the sacred fane where the worshippers were gathered, the hymn of praise gave place to cries of terror and pain. On the afternoon of the 21st October, 1638, during Divine service, a terrible thunderstorm broke over the church, of which four separate accounts, written at the time, are preserved. Two of these, which are quarto tracts, were published in London in the same year; another was written by the Rev. George Lyde, the vicar of Widecombe, who was in the pulpit; and the fourth, which is now to be seen on a wooden tablet affixed to the interior wall of the tower, was by Richard Hill, the village schoolmaster. Mr. Lyde's account of the storm, which is in rhyme, remained till recently in MS. It is very interesting, as it not only gives the particulars of the occurrence, but also a short description of the parish at that time. Mr. Hill has also given his account of the tempest in rhyme. The lines were originally painted on boards in black letter, but these becoming decayed, new ones substituted in 1786, and when we first saw them, some 30 years ago, were placed on the north wall of the chancel. They were removed to their present position when the church was undergoing restoration.

From these accounts, which do not, however, exactly agree, we gather that while the service was proceeding the church became wrapped in darkness, and to such an extent that those assembled were unable to see to read. Among others there were present one Roger Hill, 'a gentleman of good account in the parish,' and who is supposed to have been a relative of Richard Hill, the schoolmaster; Master Ralph Rouse, a vintner, of Widecombe; Robert Meade, a warrener in the employ of Sir Richard Reynolds; Mrs. Lyde, the wife of the vicar; Mrs. Ditford and Sibella Milward, and one who is described as 'a maid of Manaton, which came thither that afternoon, to see some friends.' There must indeed have been a good number at the service, for no less than sixty-two persons received injuries, and in addition four were killed.

Suddenly the silence in the darkened church was broken by a loud peal of thunder, and the lightning for an instant dispelled the gloom. Then the darkness increased until the frightened people could not see each other. Presently the church was filled, as it were, with flame, some afterwards saying they saw a great fiery ball pass through the window. The whole congregation was terrified, many falling on their knees, and some prone upon the floor of the building, while a great cry of agony arose. A pinnacle of the tower, which even then had long been the glory of the moor, was thrown down, and crashing through the roof added to the terrors of the people. But the falling masonry injured none but the 'maid of Manaton,' who Master Frynd, the coroner, said was killed by a stone. A beam fell between Mr. Lyde and the clerk, but neither was hurt. To the direct effects of the lightning were to be traced most of the injuries that were received.

Roger Hill was sitting in his seat by the chancel, when suddenly his head was dashed against the wall. He was taken from the church alive, but died that night. His son, who sat by him, was unhurt. Robert Meade was instantly killed, his skull being cloven, and his brains thrown upon the ground whole. The other victim, Sibella Milward, like Roger Hill, was carried from the church, but was so burnt by the lightning that she did not live to see another day.

The effects of the lightning were indeed strange. We are told that some had their clothes burnt, while they themselves were unhurt, and that others were scorched, while their clothing shewed no traces of burning whatever. 'Some had their stockings and legs burnt and scalded, and their outward buskins not thread-singed.' The money in the purse of one man was partly melted, also a key which hung to it, but only some minute holes were made by the lightning in the purse itself. The ruff and linen of Mrs. Lyde were burnt, and also the clothing of Mrs. Ditford. A boy who was wearing his hat in the church had one half of it cut off, but was himself not harmed; and many were thrown from their seats in the body of the church. In the midst of the terrible scene, while the thunder shook the building and the lightning flash revealed the faces of the terror-stricken men and women, a little child, who 'scarce knew good from ill,' walked heedlessly through the church, and no harm befell her.

When at length the storm had passed and calmness was in a measure restored, Master Rowse, the vintner, stood up in his place. 'Neighbours,' he said 'in the name of God shall we venture out of the church?' Mr. Lyde thought it better that they should proceed with their devotions; if death overtook them it could do so in no more fitting place. But the church was terribly rent and torn. Although the elements no longer warred against the building, danger was to be apprehended from falling walls. The words of the vicar were unheeded, and the people, thinking only of their safety, left the devastated fabric. That night, when David Barry, a serving man of the lord of one of the manors of Widecombe, ventured into the tower, he found it choked with rubbish, and the noble fane, the pride of the men of the valley, blackened and disfigured.

As time passed on, and the events of that October afternoon slowly faded from men's minds, tradition made the great thunderstorm her theme. It was related that somewhile before the darkness fell on Widecombe, and when the sky was yet blue, and the fields smiled beneath the autumn sun, a swarthy rider stopped at the door of the hostelry at Pound's Gate. He desired to be supplied with drink, and was served by the landlady herself. Raising the goblet to his lips, he slowly drained the contents, and the terrified hostess noticed that the liquor hissed as it ran down his throat, at though it had been poured upon red-hot metal. Then, protruding from beneath his long riding cloak, she noticed the foot of her strange customer, and saw that it resembled that of a goat. Handing the empty goblet to her, together with a handful of coins, the horseman inquired the way to Widecombe. With fear and trembling she directed him, and, spurring his black horse, which was impatiently pawing the ground, the mysterious stranger rode rapidly off. Arriving at Widecombe, he raised the fearful storm to wreck the house of God. But his power was limited, and ere long the damage he had wrought was repaired, and the church became again the pride of the men of the Webburn valleys and the free tenants of the Forest.

XI

THE KING'S FARMERS

When through failure of an heir to the Earldom or Dukedom of Cornwall the Forest of Dartmoor has at different periods in its history reverted to the custody of the Crown, it has not been unusual for the Monarch to bestow it temporarily upon a subject. These grantees held it on a different footing from such as were its custodians only. The former were invested with powers over it, similar to those which the Earl or the Duke possessed, while the latter acted merely as deputies of the owners. It is probable that a small sum was paid as an acknowledgement by those to whom the Forest was granted, as in the case of the Earls of Cornwall, who, as already mentioned, rendered £10 yearly for it. But such payments were not regarded as a rental. It was not until the 15th century that the older custom of grants was superseded by leases, but from 1425 onward we find several instances of the Forest being let for a term of years, and the lessees are sometimes styled the King's farmers.

We have already referred to Siward, the Dane, as being not improbably a lord of the Forest before the Conquest; and also to John, as apparently holding it before he ascended the throne. Mention has also been made of Hugh de Audley and Piers de Gaveston as having held it under grant, and of William Briwere and John Dabernan, its custodians, the one in the 13th century and the other in the 14th. Others to whom the Forest was granted were Richard de Abberbury, in 1377, who held it, in part, during his life; and Philip de Courtney, and his wife, upon whom it was bestowed by Richard II in 1388.

The Forest of Dartmoor having reverted to the Crown on the death of Edmund, Earl of Cornwall, in 1300, Edward I placed it in the custody of John de Tresympel. In his charge it remained, together with the manor of Lydford, for 7 years, when, on the accession of Edward II, both the manor and Forest were given by that Monarch to his favourite, Piers de Gaveston. They were, however, to own him for their lord but a few brief years. In 1312 he who had been the recipient of so many honours and rewards from his King, and upon whom Edward had bestowed the hand of Margaret, his niece, was led to the block at Warwick.

The manor and Forest having again come into the Crown, Thomas le Ercedekne was appointed custodian of them, and in the following year the

Bailiwick of Dartmoor was placed in the charge of Thomas de Shirigge. But it was not long held by the King, for Margaret, the widow of Gaveston, having married Hugh de Audley, Earl of Gloucester, the manor and the moor were bestowed upon them, to hold during the life of the countess. In 1319 the Forest was demised by them to the Abbot of Tavistock for 5 years, the King having empowered them to grant the lease. But although the grant to De Audley and his wife, Margaret, comprised 'the Manor of Lydford and Chase of Dartmoor,' and continued in force until the death of the latter in 1342, the King retained certain rights over it. Thus he granted the custody of De Audley's lands to Matthew de Cranthorn, and in 1327 granted 'the Bailiwick of the Forestership of Dartmoor' to Richard Caleware, his butler.

The Black Prince was lord of the Forest of Dartmoor for a period extending over 34 years, from 1342 to 1376, and it was while he held it that John Dabernan was its custodian. The latter is described as Constable of the Castle of Lydford and Custos of the Forest of Dartmoor, and is referred to by the jurors at an Inquisition taken at Chagford in 1388 as the late steward of the Lord Edward, late Prince of Wales.

In the year following that in which the death of the Black Prince occurred, Richard II granted the 'custody' of the Forest to Richard de Abberbury for the term of his life and also the profits of the herbage. Several disputes with the Duchy officers arose on the question of what his profits really were, and the Inquisition named above was ordered for the purpose of determining this. But the moneys arising from the herbage of the Forest appear to have been received by him until his death, for in a patent by which the King in 1388 granted the manor and profits of the Forest to Philip de Courtney and his wife, these profits are reserved to De Abberbury. It was not until 1399, when the death of the latter probably took place, that the herbage was given to Courtney. This was in the first of Henry IV, and by patent confirming the grant of the manor and Forest made by Richard, and securing them to the grantees for the term of their lives. But the King soon desired to regain possession of that which he had bestowed, and the gift was annulled in 1404. Twenty-one years later, in the time of Henry IV, the system of farming out the manor and the Forest was introduced.

In 1425 the custody of the Borough and manor of Lydford and the chase of Dartmoor was let to Sir Philip Courtney and Sir Walter Hungerford for 7 years, at a rent of £105. With the exception of an interval of 5 years, from 1441 to 1446, they continued to be leased until 1456, the last lessee in Henry VI's reign being Sir William Bonvile to whom they were let for 100 marks. Besides Lydford and the moor, the lease also included the manor of South Teign, in the parish of Chagford, and which was also known as the Prince's Manor. Risdon says that the tithing of South Teign was ancient demesne, but it has been considered doubtful whether it originally formed part of the lands of the Duchy.

It has already been stated that in 1626 Charles I granted a lease of the Forest to Sir Thomas Reynell for 31 years. But previous to that date, and while he was Prince of Wales, Charles had leased it to Sir Thomas, and, as it appears, the rent was in each case the same, £28. 12s. 5d. There was a covenant in the lease to discharge the Crown from all yearly payments to the foresters, herdsmen, priours, and other officers of the manor and Forest.

About this period the waste lands in Devon seem to have had more than ordinary attention directed to them. The King, according to a note among the State papers of the year 1630, formed the idea of improving Dartmoor and Exmoor, and other common lands, and it was considered that by so doing no less a sum than £100,000 in fines might be raised, and also a large yearly rent. Modern speculators have entertained similar hopes. It is fortunate that Charles did not proceed with the scheme; had he done so it is highly probable that the experience of later 'improvers' would have been his own.

Sir Thomas Reynell did not continue to hold the Forest for many years after the granting of the second lease, for in 1634 Sir Nicholas Slanning was in possession of it. From the evidence of Richard Bold, given in a suit for tithes in 1702, we learn that Sir Thomas assigned the lease to Sir Nicholas, for Bold states that he had seen the deed by which this was affected. But the original term for which the lease was granted did not run its course. The restless period of the Civil Wars followed a few years after the signing of the deed which made Sir Nicholas Slanning the farmer of the Forest, and when the strife came to an end Dartmoor was in the hands of the Parliamentarians, and its holder had fallen on the field at Bristol a victim to his loyalty.

During the Commonwealth the trustees of the Parliament leased the Forest, and the Borough of Lydford and the manor were sold by the trustees for the sale of the Crown lands. The lessee of the Forest was James Pearce, and, as is shown by a memorandum of receipt, the rent was £28. 3s. 5d. William Braddon, of Stoke Clymsland, in Cornwall, bought the Borough of Lydford in 1650, and 9 years later Thomas Menhere, of London, purchased the manor.

If the lease of Sir Nicholas Slanning had been brought to an abrupt termination, so certainly were these bargains. At the Restoration the manor and Forest were once more in the Crown, and then it was that Margaret Slanning, daughter of Sir Nicholas, petitioned the King for a lease of the Forest. It was to compensate her, she said, for the number of years her father had lost therein by the late wars. But for her loss there could be no compensation. Charles acceded to her request, and on the 1st August, 1660, a lease was granted to Richard Arundel, of Trerise, in Cornwall, in trust for her, of the Forest and the manor, and the profits of the Stannary Courts, for 31 years, at a rent of £28. 12s. 5d., and 33s. 6d. respectively, and 30s. for a mill, parcel of the Borough of Lydford.

Six years after the granting of the lease a contract was entered into by the Earl of Southampton and Lord Ashley in behalf of Charles II empowering Sir Gervase Lucas and others to treat with the commoners. This was for the purpose of carrying out a project that had been set on foot for dividing the moor between the King and others who had rights upon it. It was seriously proposed that a considerable part of it should be enclosed for his Majesty's use, and that the owners and commoners should divide the remainder between them. The reward which Sir Gervase and those who were with him were to reap for the carrying out of the scheme was a 50 years' lease in that portion of the moor the King was to reserve, at one-fourth of the clear yearly value. But the commoners had a word to say before the apportionment and enclosure of the land could be effected; and when Sir Gervase unfolded his plans to the Devonshire men, it is probable that he speedily discovered he had reckoned without his host. The project fell to the ground.

A son of Sir Nicholas Slanning was created baronet by Charles II in 1662, and he afterwards became holder of the Forest. He was succeeded by his son, Andrew, and they are both mentioned as being the King's farmers, by deponents in a suit for tithes instituted by David Birchincha, rector of Lydford. The family was connected with Dartmoor for a considerable period, dating from the Dissolution to the death of Sir Andrew Slanning, when it became extinct. The extensive manors, once the property of the abbots of Buckland, were purchased when the monks were dispersed by the representative of the family. Like the abbots, the Slannings appear to have imagined that their rights on the moor gave them greater power than was really the case. About 1567 Nicholas Slanning laid claim to the whole of Walkhampton Common, but judgement was given against him. He, however, or his immediate descendants, enclosed a considerable portion of the common, as may be seen at the present day. The jury of survey who perambulated the bounds of the Forest in 1609 refer to this.

At the death of Sir Andrew Slanning the family possessions passed to the heirs of the sister of the Sir Nicholas who fell in the fight before Bristol, and afterwards by marriage to the Heywoods. Frederick, Duke of Cornwall, and son of George II, demised the Forest to Mrs Mary Heywood and Abram Elton, for a long term of years, who licensed priours, or moormen, to take cattle to pasture, and to collect the fees. This inaugurated a new system in farming out the Forest, and one which, with some modifications, still obtains. The property remained with the Heywoods until 1798, when the manors were purchased by Mannaseh Lopes, ancestor of the present Sir Massey Lopes, of Maristowe.

Among those who held the formerly important office of Rider, or Master Forester, or Ranger of Dartmoor, may be named Sir John Dynham and Sir Walter Courtney, in the 15th century; Sir Walter Raleigh, Lord Brooke, Sir Henry Waring, and Sir Edward Hastings, in the 16th, in which century also the Earl of Bedford was appointed Custos of the Forest; the Earl of Pembroke and Sir John Grenville, in the 17th; and Sir Francis Godolphin, early in the 18th century.

XII

LIGHT FROM LAWSUITS

In the course of our remarks reference has more than once been made to the evidence of deponents in suits brought for tithe of agistment in the 17th and early in the 18th centuries. The defendants, who, in some cases, were commoners dwelling on the borders of the moor, and in others Forest men, claimed to be exempt from the payment of tithe, as a sum of £3 yearly was paid to the rector of Lydford in lieu of same, in accordance with the grant of Henry III. From the depositions taken in these suits, in which the plaintiffs appear to have been generally successful, we are able to gather much concerning the commoners and the customs of the Forest at that time, and this is all the more valuable as coming directly from yeomen and priours.

Although the rights of the Dartmoor Commoners have never been called in question, the latter have sometimes been disturbed in the exercise of them in other directions than that of demands for tithe. Thomas Taverner, of Chagford, deponent in a suit in 1627, states that he was sued about 7 years before that time in the Consistory Court of Exeter by Richard Harbyn, who, having obtained a lease of the tithes of Lydford, pretended to be the farmer of the agistment of the Forest. But Taverner petitioned the King's Council, and whether it was that the suit was stayed, or whether Harbyn withdrew, does not exactly appear, but, at all events, he heard nothing more of the demand.

Richard Harbyn may, of course, have supposed that on becoming owner of the tithes of Lydford he had a right to the agistment fees, that is presuming he had previously known nothing whatever of the usages of the moor. But this is not very probable, and that he pretended to be the farmer of the herbage, as Thomas Taverner says, is much more likely. And if so he was by no means the first who had claimed to have some control over the agistments on Dartmoor without possessing any such rights. Nearly 150 years before – in 1478 – complaint was made that one John Hawston, of Elburton, had been in the habit of yearly driving the commons in the neighbourhood of the Erme and Yealm, and a considerable portion of the south quarter of the Forest as well. The cattle which he found there at the time of his drifts he impounded in the pinfold at Torry Combe, and he was, therefore, attached to answer for his actions, which it was said resulted in damage to the lord of the Forest amounting to 40 shillings yearly.

The valley known as Torry Combe is in the parish of Shaugh, and its head is just below Tolch Bridge, on the road between Cornwood and Meavy, and not far from the Lee Moor Clay Works. The little River Torry rises at a spot called White Hill Yeo, a short distance above the bridge, and flowing through the Combe, passes onward by Newnham and Plympton St. Mary Church to mingle its waters with those of the Plym at Long Bridge. Whether the pinfold to which John Hawston drove the cattle he found on the moor was ever used as a place in which animals were gathered at the time of the authorised drifts in that district we are unable to say. The probability is that it was not, and at the period of his interference with the commoners' cattle it is nearly certain that it was not put to such a use. There is little doubt that the gathering-place for animals then found in that part of the moor was the enclosure on the left bank of the Erme at Brown Heath, a short distance outside the confines of the Forest.

Before the south quarter of the Forest was farmed, which, as we have seen, was in 1404, it is most likely that animals found at the drifts within what afterwards became its bounds, were driven to Dunnabridge Pound. When a fourth quarter was farmed there would be a separate drift for that part of the Forest, and Dunnabridge Pound being at a considerable distance, a place to which cattle could be driven, at all events in the first instance, would become requisite. Hence, there can be little doubt that the walled enclosure on the brink of the river at Brown Heath, and which is known as Erme Pound, owes its existence to the readjustment of the quarters into which the Forest is divided, and is, therefore, probably of 15th century date. There are references in the 14th century to the pasturage in the Erme Valley, and also to that in the Avon Valley near by, but we have been able to find no mention of the pound until much later.

The situation of Erme Pound renders it by far the most interesting of any of the drift pounds on Dartmoor. To him who wanders for the first time up this solitary valley, it comes as a surprise to find in a part of the moor so remote this ancient enclosure, with its substantially-built wall and its wide gateway, and the ruins of two small houses, the gable end of one of which is yet standing. These remains tell him that in this quiet spot near the river's source men once gathered, and that at times the scene was one of animation. And if report speaks truly it was one of revelry, too. We have been told by a moorman how it used to be related that broken jars and bottles of an antiquated shape were to be found at Erme Pound, particularly in and around the little houses near its gate. But the heather and the turf have grown since then, and have covered these evidences of former conviviality. At all events, during the 30 years that we have known the pound we do not remember having met with such there.

Erme Pound approaches a circular form, though the wall is irregularly built. It is 345 yards in circumference, and was evidently formed on the lines of a still older enclosure, in the same manner as was Dunnabridge Pound. Enough remains of the more ancient foundation to attest this, and the presence of hut circles confirms it. Where it is highest the wall attains a height of about 4½ feet. At the gateway it is fully 6 feet wide, one side of the entrance being faced with large blocks of stone.

Erme Pound

The enclosure to which cattle were driven when the drift was made in the north quarter of the Forest was Creber Pound, on the verge of Gidleigh Common. It is mentioned in a case that occurred when Sir Thomas Reynell farmed the Forest, and which concerns the manner of dealing with estrays. On Monday, the 15th July, 1632, a drift took place in the north quarter, and among other animals driven to Creber Pound was a black ox. There being no one present to claim it, in accordance with the usual custom, it was driven to the pound at Lydford Castle, and the fact made public. No owner being forthcoming it was adjudged to be an estray, and was forfeited to Sir Thomas as the farmer of the King's Forest. It was valued by three or four of the Forest tenants at 56s. 8d., and after the animal's ears had been cut as an estray, the reeve delivered it to William Stowel, who acted as the agent of Sir Thomas.

Animals were supposed to remain at Creber Pound for 3 days, and at Lydford until the 16th August, as estrays, the custom being to make the drifts at any time between the 23rd June and the 6th August. According to Sir Thomas Reynell's statement, animals not claimed within 8 days after the 16th August were forfeited. Presumably these rules were observed in the case of the black ox, but it would appear that the usages of the Forest demanded that something further should have been done. Oliver Warren, who it is to be supposed was the owner of the ox, brought an action against William Stowel, who had received the animal from the reeve and had retained possession of it. Warren said that after being valued the estray should have been presented at the next court at Lydford, to be held within a certain time, and that it should have been declared forfeited by the steward at that court and a record made of it.

There can scarcely be a doubt that this mode of procedure was the correct one. We cannot suppose that the reeve possessed the power to declare animals forfeited. And Oliver Warren explains why the usual course was not followed. The death of William, Earl of Pembroke, had left the Duchy without a steward, and no court was held at Lydford. Thus the reeve had dealt with matters usually adjudicated upon by the Duchy court, and it is therefore not a matter for surprise that Oliver Warren should consider he had not met with that justice to which he was entitled. How he fared in his lawsuit there appears to be nothing to tell us, which may probably mean that the matter was arranged without further litigation. But although we are in doubt as to its termination, the episode of the black ox is not without its value as throwing some light upon Forest usages and how they were sometimes observed.

Creber Pound is merely a small piece of common cut off from the moor by some enclosures, and totally unlike the other pounds on the moor. Two roads pass through it, but there are gates at the entrances, so that cattle are prevented from straying. There is another enclosure used as a drift pound for the north quarter of the forest, but for ponies only. This is Halstock Pound, and it stands on the verge of the Down of that name. It is not of great size, but the wall is high and well built.

Whether the owners of animals which had been impounded often acted as did John Coole, of Slade, on the 22nd July, 1512, we cannot say, but are not of that opinion. It appears that forty oxen and steers and ten geldings belonging to Coole had been imparked by the reeve at Brattor, which was probably the hill near Lydford village we now call Bra Tor. It does not transpire whether the animals had been taken as estrays at a drift or were found pastured on the Forest without being entered on the agistment roll; but it is certain that the proceeding did not please John Coole. Accordingly on the day named he, with fourteen others, 'unlawfully and riotously, and in the manner of an insurrection,' broke into the place where the animals were and drove them away, at the same time driving out sixteen steers impounded as estrays. Coole and those who assisted him were charged with the offence at the court at Lydford, but as neither of them dwelt within the liberty of the manor of Lydford, and had no property there that could be distrained upon, the fines imposed were never levied.

Among other matters gathered from the evidence of deponents in the tithe suits, we learn the customary manner of proceeding when it was desired to enclose a newtake. Anthony Torr, a witness in a suit brought by Thomas Bernaford, the rector of Lydford, in 1702, says that the mode of obtaining one formerly, and he believed also at that time, was for the person who was entitled as a holder of one of the ancient Forest farms to apply to the steward of the manor of Lydford, who would instruct the reeve and three holders of Forest farms to attend and measure out the ground. On this being done, the grant was made by the steward at a Duchy court, and the land was held by copy of Court Roll.

But the pasturage of the Forest seems to have been valued by the free tenants more highly than the privilege of occasionally adding a few acres to their enclosed lands. The evidence of Edward Hunt, of Lydford, given in 1627, shews such to have been the case, and other evidence given later points the same way. Still, the land-grabber was not unknown on Dartmoor in early times, and if those who were entitled to enclose did not always avail themselves of that privilege, it is equally certain that others, possessing no rights of the kind, sometimes shewed a desire to do so. In 1442 John Jeffery was ordered to be attached for having appropriated 40 acres of land to his own use, between Badworthy and Manger Ford, on the North Teign; and in 1468 Reginald Cole was summoned with others to answer the King for enclosing 200 acres of the pasture between the Erme and the Avon.

And attempts were not only made to steal land, but also to evade payment of agistment fees. In 1444 Robert Breston was attached for having cattle pastured on the moor without being entered on the agistment roll, and in 1632 Sir Thomas Reynell brought an action against three owners of cattle, who, he says, pastured great numbers of sheep, beasts, and colts in the Forest and took them away before the drifts, thus defrauding him of his profit.

From evidence given in 1702 we find that the yearly rent from the whole of the ancient Forest farms amounted to £9. 15s. 1d., and that the rent derivable from the newtakes was £1. 10s. The services which the tenants are called upon to render are also set forth, together with the agistment fees at that time. The Forest tenants are all admitted at the Court of the Manor, and some of the ancient customs are still preserved. Mr W. Burt, in his preface to Carrington's poem, refers to the manner in which the act of seizin on surrenders has always been made. It is by delivering a mote of reed, which, as Mr. Burt says, is remarkable in a district not productive of grain.

In the evidence of Walter Williams, given in 1689, the custom followed at coroners' inquests is set forth. Williams, who dwelt in the parish of Lydford, and who at the date named was 70 years of age, says that when any 'strange corpse is found dead' in the Forest, it was usual to choose six men from the Borough of Lydford, and six others from the Forest as a jury, and that the oldest man in the borough was always coroner. He further states that about 40 years before that time he was chosen one of such a jury, and that the charge of burying the body at Lydford was borne equally by the inhabitants of the borough and the Forest. Walter Williams speaks of this as an ancient custom, and that it was so is proved by a document of the time of Henry VIII, headed 'Instruccons for my Lorde Prynce,' in which the following occurs:– 'And yf a man dye by mysfortune or be slayne wtin the said Forest, Mores and waste the Crowner of Lydeforde shall crowne and sytte vpon hym.'

We also learn from witnesses in the tithe suits that early in the 17th century it became customary for the holders of the Forest farms to temporarily enclose parcels of land, and till them for a year or two. Then they were suffered to lie open again, and once more became common land. This was done by licence of the King, or the Duke, or the farmer of the Forest, and a rent of 2 shillings an acre was paid while the land was under tillage.

It is also stated that the reeve was then chosen yearly out of the Forest holders, and was obliged to attend at each of the courts held at Lydford, and failing to do so was liable to be fined by the steward. One witness deposes that it was within his knowledge that a fine of 40 shillings had been imposed upon a reeve for not making his appearance at a court.

The priours, or moormen, as they were beginning to be called in the 17th century, are described by William Torre, of Widecombe, as poor men. They lived in the Forest, and were tenants of the holders of the ancient farms. These were evidently the descendants of the older herdsmen, or censers, who, as we have already seen, were permitted to have a liberty of the Forest in very early times.

The references to the rectors of Lydford and to others who claimed tithes by witnesses in the suits brought to recover them are both interesting and amusing. William Pellowe, of Lydford, speaks of William Barber, the parson there in 1627, as a man of honest conversation, who demeaned himself well, and was attentive to his duties as a preacher. He kept a good house for the entertainment of his neighbours and the poor, the latter being often relieved by him, and he was especially mindful of children. Not quite so flattering was the description of Andrew Gove, rector of Peter Tavy in 1665 who was accused of a desire to 'wrest and distort' tithes out of a greedy aim, and still less so was that of Richard Pote, rector of Lydford in 1682. In that year Michael Mann, John Hext, and William French, men of Widecombe, filed a bill against Richard Pote to restrain him from bringing suits of law for tithes of pasture in the Forest. They said they had always been exempted from the payment of such, 'but that Pote, well knowing in his own conscience and by long observation that tithes in kind are not due, nevertheless out of a surly and a greedy mind and humour and covetous desire to wrest and extort from them tithes which he well knows do not belong to him, brings suits at law, and they pray that he may be restrained.'

The question of tithes of pasturage appears to have long been a vexed one, for as early as 1479 John Billek, the vicar of Walkhampton, was attached to answer to the lord of the Forest for that he was 'a common disturber and vexer of the tenants of the Lord the Prince in the Spiritual Courts for tithes of cattle and beasts pasturing in the Common of Devon, next and around the Forest of the Lord the Prince of Dartmoor, contrary to the custom of the liberty of the common aforesaid, to the great prejudice of the Lord.'

A feature of considerable value in the depositions taken in these suits for tithe, is the naming of the Forest bounds by many yeomen and priours. It is true that not one of them is able to mention the objects marking the boundary line throughout the whole of its course, but each can speak of it at certain points, and by piecing their evidence together we learn how the line was then considered to run. And in this knowledge or want of knowledge, the deponents counterpart is found in the moorman of today. We have known many, but never yet met one who was acquainted with the boundary line of the Forest except where it happened to define the quarter in which he was interested, and that part of it he generally knew well.

Some of these 17th and 18th century witnesses are not quite correct in naming the bounds, and one of them, the before-mentioned Anthony Torr, who is described as of Bishop's Tawton, seems to have mixed up the line dividing the west from the south quarter with the line of the Forest, but speaking generally the bounds given by the deponents agree with those named in the Survey of 1609.

XIII

THE PASSING OF THE OLD ORDER

Here lies Poor Old Ned,
On his last Mattress bed,
During life he was honest and free;
He knew well the Chace
But has now run his Race
And his Name was Collins D've see.
... December, 1780, aged 77.

Holne Church

In the churchyard of the little moorland village of Holne is a gravestone of slate, bearing an inscription so worn as to be in places almost indecipherable, but which upon a close examination will prove to be commemorative of one Edward Collins, and may, with care, be read as we have set it down.

Who this son of the Dartmoor borderland was, whose age over-ran man's allotted span by 7 years, and who found his last resting-place in the shadow of the sanctuary planted midway up the great hill that rises from the moor's chief river to the bold sweep of Holne Lea there is nothing to show. But the few simple facts upon the stone, nevertheless, give us some clue as to the manner of man he was. We can well believe him to have been one who always tried to do what he conceived to be his duty, but whose nature would not allow him to take too serious a view of life. A true sportsman, he knew the marks of a 'warrantable deer,' was acquainted with every fox holt in Holne Chase, every pool between Hembury Wood and Dartmeet, or on the Webburns, in which an otter was likely to be found, and always 'knew by' a badger. A favourite with all on the countryside.

We are not aware whether Edward Collins was born at Holne, and consequently known as a child to Nicholas Hunt, who was vicar there from 1699 until 1709. But we do know that during his life Holne, where at all events he must have spent many years, saw no less than seven vicars, and in all probability, John Mogridge, the latest of these, spoke the last words at his graveside. We know, too, that when they laid him to rest the festival of Christmas had not long passed, and the trees of the chase were bare, and the scant herbage on the hills brown and crisp, for in the parish register of burials for the year 1780 may be seen the words, 'December 29, Edward Collings.'

It is obvious we can say but little concerning this old borderer, but we mention him here as his life was spread over the greater part of that century, the closing years of which witnessed the old order of things on Dartmoor passing away. Born not long after Queen Anne ascended the throne, and living during the reigns of the first and second Georges, and for 20 years in that of the third, Edward Collins saw much on Dartmoor in his manhood that was not quite the same as he remembered in his youth, and when at length old age crept upon him many things wore yet another aspect. But in this there were hardly to be recognised evidences of an impending change. It was, in a measure, a transitional period during which Edward Collins lived, and yet had only matters of a kindred nature to those he witnessed since taken place, the moor would have remained today much as it had been for many years before his time. That which was to effect by far the greatest alteration in its condition came rather suddenly, and was wrought by those who dreamed they could change the face of the old Forest with the plough. But Edward Collins saw nothing of these visionary schemes, though it is possible he may have heard rumours of them. He was laid in his grave in the very year the first attempts at cultivating the great waste were made by modern 'improvers,' passing away when the old order on Dartmoor was about to end.

One of the changes that took place during the lifetime of this old sportsman of Holne Chase is found in the manner of farming out the Forest. When Mrs. Heywood and Abram Elton, who, as already stated, held it on a lease from Frederick, son of George II, licensed moormen in the four quarters to receive cattle to pasture, the first step leading to the present system of subletting was taken. Afterwards the Duchy authorities themselves adopted the plan of leasing the quarters singly and this is still continued. They are taken sometimes by moormen, and sometimes by others who sub-let them to the former. In the cases where moormen lease them direct from the Duchy, and carry on the business of receiving animals to pasture, they also sub-let the right to other moormen to do the same.

Mining on Dartmoor had for some time been in a declining state when Edward Collins was born, nor did it revive during his time. Near the head waters of the West Webburn, however, there were probably mines at work, for in the parish register of Widecombe is to be found mention of those who followed the occupation of seeking for ore. Among the entries of burials in 1710 is one of Alice, wife of John Farrant, a tinner, and in the following year the burial of Edward Wills, a tinner, is recorded. Other workings in the neighbourhood about that time were at Cator, some 7 miles or more from Holne, and at Huntingdon, on the Avon, and just within the Forest. The bounds of the former were presented for registration at the Stannary Court at Chagford in 1754, and those of the latter at the Stannary Court at Ashburton in 1759.

But the balmy days of the tin-seeker on the moor had gone by; the industry in the 18th century was but a shadow of its former state. While Edward Collins was hunting the fox and the badger in Holne Chase the tinners were turning their backs upon Dartmoor. Their ancient Parliament met for the last time on Crockern Tor in the days when the sportsman 'honest and free' thought only of meeting the staghounds at the top of Skea Wood. Ten years before he died, if we may trust one who wrote in 1770, the tin miner was hardly known in Devon.

But possibly Edward Collins, if he did not see the streamer busily at work round Holne, saw another industry of a more homely description carried on in the little village, and one which has since died out. In his time the woollen trade, though somewhat on the decline, was yet an important industry in many of the towns of Devon. About the middle of the 18th century Exeter is said to have been the greatest wool market in England, the weekly sales on a Friday averaging £10,000. Much of the cloth was woven at Crediton, which town was in a highly prosperous condition till the great fire of 1743 destroyed more than half of it, the yarn being spun in Cornwall and in the moorland villages. We may, therefore, very well suppose that Holne had its share of this spinning industry, and that the wheel was often to be seen during fine weather at the open cottage door. And the more especially as the neighbouring town of Buckfastleigh has from an early period been a seat of the woollen manufacturer, which was probably introduced there by the Cistercian monks.

Since there was a market so near at hand as Buckfastleigh, the partial destruction of the town of Crediton would not interfere with the yarn-spinners of Holne, though there is no doubt the disastrous occurrence formed the absorbing topic of conversation for a time. But there was another event in the same year, though of a totally different character, that concerned them more.

This was the placing of five bells in the tower of their church, as we may see by the date, 1743, which they bear. Edward Collins was 40 years of age when they were hung, and till his death their music struck upon his ear, alternating with that of the hounds.

Away down in the valley of the Dart, beyond the wooded hill of Hembury, rose the ruins of Buckfast Abbey, which Edward Collins must often have looked upon as he pursued the otter down the stream. Although dismantled, the vandal had not then completed his work, and much was left of the great pile, to which William Slade, one of its abbots, famed for his learning, had added, in the 15th century, some fair buildings. The ruins may not have been as in Risdon's time, who tells us they were then such as to 'move the beholders both to wonder and pity,' but they were by no means scanty. Edward Collins saw them as they are represented in Buck's view, taken about 1760, when there was sufficient remaining of the great Cistercian house whence Gabriel Doune had been ousted at the Dissolution, to show something of what it once had been. But the finishing stroke in its demolition was not put until the 'improver' of the enlightened 19th century came upon the scene. Down to about 1806 the hoary walls of the Abbey Church, and some few of its offices, were standing. Then they were taken down by those who saw in the remains nothing of value beyond what they would fetch as material for building. Whether Edward Collins had any poetry in his nature we do not know. If so, one can scarcely lament that he was resting 'on his last mattress bed' when this act of vandalism was committed.

We can quite imagine that Edward Collins took a leading part in the villagers' sports in the Play Park, as the field in which they were held was called, and which name it still bears. The principal holiday was kept on Old Midsummer-day, the chief feature in it being the roasting of a ram, and in this we may probably trace a survival of a heathen sacrifice. Formerly it was the custom for a number of the villagers to make their way to Holne Moor on the morning of the festive day, and the first ram they were able to capture became the victim. This part of the ceremony seems to have some connection with the drifts which, as we have already seen, were made on the moor at this season of the year. In fact, it would appear that Old Midsummer-day was often chosen for the purpose. Mrs. Bray, writing in 1832, says that on that day the moor farmers rode about and laid hands on all stray cattle and sheep that they could find, and drove them to the pound. This was evidently the drift, but Mrs. Bray not being acquainted with the customs of the Forest, did not apparently fully recognise the meaning of the proceeding.

On the ram being captured it was taken to the Play Park, which field is the property of the Church feoffees, killed, and roasted whole. Then the sports commenced, everybody feeling assured that should the exercise in which they indulged be productive of appetite, there was that at hand to satisfy it, and, we may be sure, no lack of nut-brown home-brewed. In later years the summary proceeding of seizing a ram on the moor gave place to one more in accordance with modern notions, and an animal was purchased, the villagers subscribing for the purpose. The scene of the revelry was also changed from the Play Park to the common.

Among those whom Edward Collins met on the festive occasions many were no doubt descendants of the early settlers in the Forest; men who had come down from Runnage and Pizwell, from Hartland and from Meripit, to join in the sports, and to taste a morsel of the roasted ram, if, indeed, morsel they were contented with. And their names were the same as we find in the Forest and its purlieus now – French, Hext, Cleave, Caunter, Coaker, and Mann, the first two being borne by

Forest tenants nearly 600 years ago.

Of many other old-time customs was Edward Collins the witness, for they had not begun to disappear in his day. Had it even been otherwise it is nearly certain he would have regretted the fact much less than he deplored the disappearance of the deer. He who knew Holne Chase so well, and the slopes of Hembury, and Brook Wood and Skea, and the valley of Dean Burn, must have seen that year by year the herds grew smaller, and that the time was coming when there would be no more work for the staghounds which were kennelled so near his home. Good Master Lyde, when he penned his lines on Widecombe in 1638, did not forget to tell of the deer that browsed on the sides of the valley. And it is certain that the coverts of Widecombe, and the woods of Holne and Scoriton, which in Henry III's time was 'stored with stags,' were among the latest of the places where they harboured on the confines of the moor. In Edward Collins's youthful days there is no doubt that many a lordly stag was roused in that country of hill and wood, but these became fewer as he grew older. Still, we may well believe that even when the prime of life was long past he saw the hounds of Bidlake Henring bring down more than one sobbing deer. But he outlived them all, though not long. The last was killed in September, 1780, and 3 months later the old man died.

And now we turn from the quiet churchyard in which on that winter day they laid Edward Collins to rest, and pass slowly up the hill to the moor. Ere reaching the gate that opens upon it, we turn to look on the scene below, for it is one that cannot be surpassed in Devon. There are the tors above the vale of Widecombe, their rugged crests standing out boldly against the sky, and the huge mass of Hameldon rising between them and the Forest; the Buckland Woods creeping up towards the commons above the windings of the Dart; and the chase which Edward Collins knew and loved so well. It is a beautiful picture, even beheld on a chilly December day, like that on which they buried the old sportsman, and brightened only by the feeble rays of the winter sun.

We pass on to the moor, and a few steps hide all these beauties from us, the wide, bare heath being alone visible. And not for long is that even so, for the day is nearly done, and in the gathering twilight the forms of furze bush and rook become indistinct, and our path is obscured. A sound as of voices is borne upon the breeze that sweeps across the waste, but it is only the moaning of the Dart, as he forces his way through the ravine yonder. Still we listen, for the river and the wind seem to speak to us, and unfold a tale of other times. In the echoes of the hills we hear the story of the ancient Forest that stretches from the borderland on which we stand far away into the darkness.

> The murmurs of the night wind come
> Across the lonely fell,
> And mingling with the river's cry,
> The Forest story tell.
> We listen to the voices low,
> Like whispers from above,
> Something of this old land to know,
> And knowing is to love.

*****

*****